From the desk of LYNDEE — *Lyndee Montgomery*

Handwritten notes:

TEAM — FULL TIME / 8 HR DAY
TIME: 10% PROD BACKLOG GROOMING
10%-20% PROF/TEAM DEV
5% SPRINT PLANNING
5% SPRINT REVIEW/RETRO

The Enterprise and Scrum

Ken Schwaber

PUBLISHED BY
Microsoft Press
A Division of Microsoft Corporation
One Microsoft Way
Redmond, Washington 98052-6399

Library of Congress Control Number: 2007926318

Printed and bound in the United States of America.

1 2 3 4 5 6 7 8 9   QWT   2 1 0 9 8 7

Distributed in Canada by H.B. Fenn and Company Ltd.

A CIP catalogue record for this book is available from the British Library.

Microsoft Press books are available through booksellers and distributors worldwide. For further information about international editions, contact your local Microsoft Corporation office or contact Microsoft Press International directly at fax (425) 936-7329. Visit our Web site at www.microsoft.com/mspress. Send comments to mspinput@microsoft.com.

Acquisitions Editor: Ben Ryan
Project Editor: Kathleen Atkins
Copy Editor: Roger LeBlanc
Editorial and Production Services: ICC Macmillan Inc.

Cover Illustration by John Hersey

Body Part No. X13-24184

Dedicated to ScrumMasters

I thank those who reviewed the book while it was in progress and made many helpful suggestions. They are Mike Cohn, Pete Deemer, Bas Vodde, Colin Bird, Kate VanBuren, Alan Buffington, and Clinton Keith. I especially thank my wife, Christina, who read, commented, and edited late into many nights.

Contents at a Glance

Table of Contents

What do you think of this book? We want to hear from you!

Microsoft is interested in hearing your feedback so we can continually improve our books and learning resources for you. To participate in a brief online survey, please visit:

www.microsoft.com/learning/booksurvey/

Part II   Start Using Scrum for Enterprise Work

Introduction

This book is for those who want to use Scrum throughout their enterprise for product development. Right now, you might have pockets within your enterprise that use Scrum, and they are more effective than elsewhere. You are at least partially convinced that using Scrum throughout the enterprise might be a way to make the whole enterprise more effective, but you could use some help in figuring out how to do so. This book is for you.

There are many reasons why your enterprise can't develop and deploy products and systems as rapidly, inexpensively, and with the quality that you would like. You and your staff probably can already list many of them. Scrum won't solve them. Scrum is simply a tool that will relentlessly and ruthlessly expose them. As you try to build product within the Scrum framework, every time one of these impediments is reached, it will be exposed in a somewhat painful way. You can then prioritize it and systematically eliminate it. When the impediments are mostly gone, Scrum is a framework that will enable the product development you desire. And it will continue to be your watchdog against any new impediment or old impediments returning home for a visit.

I've gathered quite a few experiences and stories as I've worked with enterprises adopting Scrum. In this book, I've organized them into guidance in the areas that are most problematic. Sometimes this is descriptive; other times I relate the guidance through stories. It is OK that there is no guidance in the other areas. The enterprise should figure out what is likely to work best for itself and try to use it. To the extent that an approach doesn't work, change it and change it again so that it works better and continues to work better.

Scrum does not prescribe. Scrum includes general guidelines about how to do development and principles to be applied when these recommendation are insufficient. What does this mean? This means that people have to learn to think differently. We want rules to follow, but life and product development are too complex for a single set of rules to suffice in all circumstances. You have to rely on decentralized decision-making, because there probably isn't one answer for every team any more than there is for every enterprise.

The first three chapters lay out the plan for adopting Scrum. The next two chapters provide insights into some habits that impede adoption and how some enterprises have coped with them. The remaining chapters provide techniques for solving some of the knottier issues. These will help you, but your enterprise's adoption will be different from anyone else's adoption. The only common ingredient is people, for better and worse. When people rise to the occasion and work heroically in teams, nothing is better. When they prefer to lay back, play politics, and undercut each other, nothing is worse. You'll get to see both, because Scrum will relentlessly expose everything as you proceed.

Not every enterprise that tries to adopt Scrum will succeed. At times, you and your people will hate Scrum. However, don't shoot it. It is only the messenger. To the extent that you and your enterprise succeed, though, you will always know where you stand. You will know what you can do and can't do. Sometimes such transparency let's us see things that aren't what we wish to see. However, I find knowledge preferable to uncertainty and ignorance. The goal is for you and everyone in your enterprise to wake up looking forward to coming to work, and for your competitors to wish they had never woken up.

Part I
Adopting Scrum

This first section describes how an enterprise can adopt Scrum. Learning to use Scrum would be pretty simple and straightforward if we didn't have habits to do things differently. Fitting it into our enterprises, also, would be pretty straightforward if we already weren't organized and acculturated to do things differently.

Changing enterprise habits and culture is required to get the benefits of Scrum. In this section, we assess whether those benefits are of enough value for you to go through the effort. Then we look at how to initiate an enterprise transition project. This project uses Scrum to optimize your enterprise's ability to build and deploy products. We then look at some of the changes that an enterprise encounters to get the benefits.

The chapters in this section are briefly described in the following list:

- Chapter 1, "What Do We Have to Do to Adopt Scrum?" describes how to assess whether Scrum has enough value to your enterprise for you to proceed.

- Chapter 2, "Scrum qua Scrum," describes steps to initiate Scrum within your enterprise.

- Chapter 3, "The First Year," describes the first year of adopting Scrum.

- Chapter 4, "Against Muscle Memory—The Friction of Change," describes some of the most entrenched habits that impede productivity.

- Chapter 5, "Enterprises in Transition," describes some adoption projects at several enterprises. Read these in anticipation of and preparation for your enterprise's transition, for which guidance is provided in Section 2.

Chapter 1
What Do We Have to Do to Adopt Scrum?

Consider Scrum as part of the game of product and software development. Scrum lays out the playing field and rules for the game. Your enterprise has the players for the game. They go on the field and start playing against the competition. If they are skilled, it shows. If they don't yet work as a team, don't understand the rules, or have any other flaw in their capabilities, it is painfully obvious. Everyone on the team knows what improvements are needed—more coaching, more training, better teamwork.

When Scrum is used throughout an enterprise, we have an enterprise-wide game of product development. Coordination is more important than it would be if just a single team was playing, and it's harder to achieve. (Keep in mind that a single department could have 100 teams.) Again, though, Scrum helps everyone understand what needs to be improved. Every time product development occurs, Scrum rewards excellence and exposes inadequacies.

Scrum adoption has two aspects. First, Scrum is rolled out. You teach everyone how to play the game of product development using Scrum. You teach them how to work together in small teams. This stage takes six to twelve months. The second aspect is everyone in the enterprise improving their game so that they are the best possible enterprise of teams working together. During this time, we improve skills, teamwork, and everything needed for excellence. Every time we play Scrum, we can clearly see how good we've become and what we need to do to get better. To get really, really good requires three to five years of continued improvement through using Scrum in an enterprise. Staying really good and perfecting skills is an ongoing endeavor.

Your use of Scrum will expose every reason why your enterprise has trouble building products. Scrum will keep exposing the problems until they are fixed. Scrum does this within the simple framework of building increments of software, iteration by iteration, or Sprint by Sprint. The rules, roles, and time-boxes of Scrum are few and simple. Whenever they cause a conflict with existing practices, an impediment has been encountered and made visible. The enterprise has to choose whether to change to remove the impediment or to give up on some of the benefits.

Scrum Requires a New Enterprise Culture

The Scrum paradigm embraces change, unpredictability, and complexity as inescapable constants in all product development. This complexity and unpredictability renders detailed long-term predictive plans meaningless and a waste of money. With Scrum, a vision of a project's value is projected in a baseline plan. The project moves forward, Sprint by Sprint, toward the vision. Increments are inspected every Sprint. Adaptations are then made to the project to optimize the likelihood of realizing the value.

Adventure Works, a game producer in San Diego, was the first in its industry to benefit from Scrum. Joris Kalz, Adventure Works' CTO, attended one of the very first Scrum certification sessions in 2003. Enthusiastically, he went back to Adventure Works and adopted the Scrum paradigm. His story is one of insight, persistence, and hard work. The Adventure Works story is one of culture shock and then redemption.

The product that was developed using Scrum was Vosod. It began to emerge in high-quality, regular increments. Joris adopted a sustainable pace of work, one of Scrum's practices. Everyone worked eight-hour days. Some people might look at that practice and think, "Oh, that means developers get out of working hard for the company!" Quite the contrary—a sustainable pace yields higher productivity and quality products.

Adventure Works was owned by a Japanese company. The Scrum practice of eight-hour work-days was unacceptable to the senior members of the Japanese management. They demanded longer hours, and the 12-hour work days that were normal prior to Scrum were restored. Defects rose 60 percent over the next several Sprints, more than offsetting the delivery of increased functionality. Joris restored Scrum's eight-hour workdays. When the Japanese managers in San Diego drove by the offices night after night, they again saw empty parking lots and darkened offices. This was intolerable to them. They reported to headquarters that employees at Adventure Works were indifferent and lazy. They recommended selling the company. The delivery of increments of high-quality software was good, but that was insignificant compared to the perceived sloth and cultural conflict.

The Japanese parent company sold Adventure Works to its American management in a management buyout. The parent company was glad to get rid of it. Two months later, Vosod was completed and ready to ship. Adventure Works sold Vosod to a game publisher for twice the price of the buyout. Did it make sense for the Japanese owners to sell the company when they did? Of course not, but the twisting paths of change often don't make sense. People and culture are involved—people who have feelings, beliefs, perceptions, and vested interests that cloud their perceptions.

Prove to Yourself That It Is Worth the Effort

The effort required to adopt Scrum is huge, and only enterprises with compelling reasons will make the effort. Your reason for adopting it might be unacceptable costs, missing functionality, inability to deliver software, customers going to other providers, developers leaving, lengthening release cycles, or your enterprise's increasing inability to compete. Another compelling reason is Scrum offers a significantly better way of building products.

Before you attempt an enterprise-wide adoption, you must believe that your enterprise has serious problems to fix and that Scrum is the tool to help you. The first step in gaining this belief is to use Scrum on several projects. Scrum is simple enough to understand from books (some of which are listed in Appendix B), but some initial ScrumMaster and Scrum training might be helpful. (Scrum terminology is fully defined in Appendix B.) Such training is available through *www.scrumalliance.org*. Select some high-value, high-risk initial work. Conduct a combined iteration planning meeting (called a *Sprint Planning Meeting*) and training session. Then start Sprinting. Conduct at least three Sprints. You will see value. You will clearly know the progress of a project and be able to easily accommodate changes. In addition, you will see increased productivity.

You have now seen Scrum's value on some simple projects. Now go for the jugular. Select another project—one that is difficult or one that the enterprise is having problems with. Prove to yourself that Scrum solves some of your most knotty problems. Identify several pieces of important functionality, which is enough to get going. This is the basis of the Product Backlog. Form a Scrum team and have them Sprint several times. When they've done that, the functionality should have the desired security characteristics, performance capabilities, and user experience as the finished product. Extrapolate the cost of the functionality in the third Sprint to get an estimate for the entire project. You have to wait until the third Sprint for people on the team to know each other and the system they are developing well enough to get a meaningful extrapolation.

If you are concerned whether a commercially available package works as claimed, subject it to the same process. Have Scrum teams build several pieces of high-value, tricky functionality in the package. Get early information on whether the package works as you need it to work.

Formally train people in Scrum for these projects. Courses are offered by the Scrum Alliance (*www.scrumalliance.org*) that will help them gain the needed skills. Just like in baseball, a little coaching helps a novice rapidly gain skills and technique.

Assess the Type of Change That Will Occur

You should now be convinced that Scrum can help your enterprise reach its goals. Before you proceed with adopting Scrum, however, you should consider the types of changes that other enterprises have gone through. These changes have repeatedly been more extensive than other enterprises anticipated because everyday practices are exposed as impediments. You can expect the following changes and challenges:

Staff turnover will occur. Twenty-percent turnover is common. Some people say, "I don't like this. I just want to come to work, be told what to do, and go home at the end of the day not worrying about it." We've changed the ground rules with Scrum. People are asked to commit to solving problems in teams. Some people might not want this type of work.

The third through ninth months of the change will be particularly difficult. Problems and dysfunctions that have always existed in your enterprise will be highlighted at this stage. They haven't been fixed yet because they are particularly entrenched or difficult. Solutions have been hard to devise or achieve. When Scrum again highlights them, others on the project might wonder why they ever embarked on the Scrum process. At this point, look back and observe the progress that has been made. Projects are moving forward, software is being delivered, risks are being identified and removed, and people are working together. You will have the courage to continue moving forward only by looking back at the progress made.

Conflict will occur. Expect conflict. Conflict is a sign of change. People have different opinions about how things should be done. A new way of operating must be conceived. Because many enterprises discourage conflict, people might not be skilled at resolving conflict. People need to be trained to resolve conflicts.

Product management's job will change and will be harder. Product managers and customers are now Product Owners. They are responsible for managing the projects, Sprint by Sprint, to maximize value and control risk. They are accountable to senior management for the success or failure of the project. They are the single, wringable neck. If members of senior management want to find out how a project is doing, they will call the Product Owner. They will no longer call engineering or a project manager.

Engineering is accountable for quality. The engineering organization is responsible for figuring out how to build and deploy a quality increment every Sprint. The quality will be the same as that needed in the final product. The ScrumMaster will not allow them to lower quality to increase productivity.

Compensation policies need to change. Scrum is about team heroics, not individual heroics. The majority of the enterprise's bonus and incentive funds need to be allocated based on the team's performance rather than the individual's performance. If a team does really well, reward everyone on the team.

Jobs will change. Some existing jobs will disappear, and people will fulfill new roles. For instance, a project manager might become a ScrumMaster. A functional manager will no longer have a function to manage and might become a ScrumMaster or Product Owner. Career paths become far less important than contribution to the team and the enterprise.

Management's primary responsibility will shift from command to servant leadership.[1] Managers are responsible for the performance of their area of the enterprise. Their usual tactics are to direct and command. They figure out what needs to be done and tell people who work for them to do it. This hierarchically decomposes until the bottom person is actually doing the work. With Scrum, management's responsibilities remain the same, but the philosophy and techniques change. Managers will lead and serve their staffs to achieve their goals. They will remove impediments. They will guide, train, coach, mentor, and get their people to do the best they can. Their role is very much like a parent: to grow their people so that they are mature and self-managing These attributes are best learned through study and experience, not by being told what to do.

Management turnover will occur. Management is going to be asked to go through significant changes. (See the change details in the preceding paragraph.) They will do extremely difficult work over the next several years. Some managers won't want to. Up to 20 percent of them might leave as they find that they don't like the new way of working and managing.

More people might not be the answer. When we want more work done, we often hire more people. This is well documented as an ineffective approach.[2] Adding people to productive teams or diluting the ranks of existing skilled people by spreading them among new teams reduces both measured productivity and quality. In my experience, Scrum's self-managing teams generate at least 50-percent productivity improvement in the first year of use, and more thereafter. Focus on implementing Scrum, not adding more people.

Caveats

You probably have tried to implement new processes before. Please remember that Scrum is less a process than a tool for you to build processes appropriate to your enterprise. Like any tool, there are right ways and wrong ways to use it. Two caveats that you should keep in mind when using Scrum are as follows:

Do not change Scrum. Scrum isn't a process that you modify to fit your enterprise. Instead, it exposes every dysfunction in your enterprise while you build products. It is your canary in a coal mine.[3] Whenever people change Scrum, it's because they have run into a problem, dysfunction, or conflict that they do not want to face and fix. Instead, they change Scrum so that the problem remains invisible and remains deadly to your enterprise. If you allow this to happen, you will have just lost Scrum's primary benefit.

---

1   James Autry, *The Servant Leader* (Three Rivers Press, 2004)

2   Frederick Brooks, *The Mythical Man Month* (Addison Wesley, 1995)

3   Coal miners placed canaries in the mines they worked in because canaries are more sensitive to carbon monoxide than people. When a canary died, it was time to get out of the mine.

Do not wait. This book contains recommendations, such as starting Scrum projects or having meetings. Do not wait to get things in place before starting. Start immediately. Once you've started, the most important impediments to remove are identified in the heat of the moment— the impediments that you wanted to "get in place" prior to starting. There is a tendency in enterprises to wait, to plan, to overthink. Scrum forces you to act, to build things of value, and to look in the mirror and see your dysfunctions. Acta non verba.

If you have thought about these changes, considered their impact on your enterprise, and still want to proceed, the next chapters are for you.

Chapter 2
Scrum qua Scrum

You decided to proceed. Excellent! First, I'll describe the adoption process. Then I'll describe the kickoff meeting for initiating it.

You use three types of Scrum teams to adopt Scrum. The first type is a single Scrum team responsible for managing the adoption. This team is called the *Enterprise Transition team*, or *ETC*. The second type of Scrum team is responsible for doing the adoption work and causing the enterprise to change. These teams are called *Scrum rollout teams*. The third type of Scrum team builds products for the enterprise using Scrum. They are called *Scrum development teams*. These teams are fully described in the Scrum literature. All of these teams use the Scrum process to achieve their goals. We'll cover the first two in some detail in this chapter.

An enterprise's senior management is the ETC Scrum team. The most senior executive in the enterprise is the Product Owner. A Scrum Product Owner is responsible for directing the work of a Scrum team. He or she does so from a list of work, the Product Backlog, that always directs teams to do the highest value work next. This is the person who can cut through organizational, departmental, and personal conflicts for the good of the whole enterprise. The Product Owner's stakeholders are everyone in the enterprise. The ETC team ScrumMaster holds ETC together and keeps it going using Scrum. He or she is the person responsible for the Scrum process being used correctly. He or she must be a full-time, respected, and capable person within the enterprise who has a deep knowledge of the enterprise. He or she must have determination to make Scrum adoption happen and an ability to work with people. The rest of the ETC team consists of the heads of development, human resources, administration, and finance. If this is an enterprise that develops products and sells them externally, the heads of product management, marketing, and sales are included in the team. If this is an enterprise that uses the products internally, the head of the business units that use the products and cause them to be built are included in the team.

The ETC Scrum team commits to a goal every iteration, or Sprint. The team members then work with each other and do whatever is necessary to reach that goal. The goal of the team transcends the goals of any individual team member. Individual success of top executives transcending team success can result in the failure to change the enterprise. The ETC Scrum team can succeed in transforming the enterprise through the use of Scrum only if its members work together to reach the project goals. Change can't happen without this type of teamwork, from the top management levels of the enterprise through every Scrum team. Team members need to trust each other to effect change, and they need to be ready to openly have conflict to reach the best solutions possible. An excellent primer for this type of team work is *The Five Dysfunctions of a Team* by Patrick Lencioni (Josey-Bass, 2002). This book is an easy read that I recommend for the members of any Scrum team, but especially the ETC Scrum team.

A prioritized list of work that needs to be done drives the adoption. This list is called the *Transition Product Backlog (TPB)*. TPB is a type of Product Backlog, but its product is a changed enterprise. TPB items are defined by the ETC team and also arise from Scrum development teams, as they encounter impediments. The highest priority item in the TPB is to kick off some product development projects using Scrum. *Do this immediately, without any delay.* The rest of the TPB is the work required to adopt Scrum. Some of it rolls Scrum out to all projects and programs. Some of it is organizational, engineering, and product management changes. Some of it is the work needed to remove impediments, resolve conflicts, and make changes.

The ETC Scrum team creates Scrum rollout teams to perform the tasks related to the enterprise change called for by the highest priority TPB work. Rollout team members might come from management or other sources. Team members don't have to work full time on the rollout team. However, their availability and competence will dictate the pace of the Scrum adoption and enterprise change. Each team appoints its own ScrumMaster. One member of the ETC team will be the Product Owner for each team during each Sprint.

Figure 2-1 shows the organization of ETC.

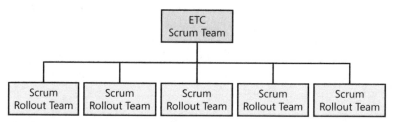

Figure 2-1   Enterprise transition project organization

The ETC Sprints are two weeks long. At the start of a Sprint, a rollout team selects high-value TPB items. The goal of the Sprint is for the rollout team to remove these impediments and to create enterprise change that optimizes productivity and effectiveness. These Sprints are shorter than Sprints for Scrum development teams, whose Sprints are normally one-month long. The shorter length allows the ETC team to more closely monitor enterprise changes and their impact. Each Scrum rollout team has a daily Scrum. The ETC Scrum team also has a daily Scrum in which it provides guidance and help to the rollout teams. ScrumMasters on development projects might also come to the ETC daily Scrum to ask for help in removing important impediments to their team's progress.

Scrum rollout teams can either be ongoing or formed by the ETC Scrum team prior to a Sprint Planning Meeting. These rollout teams meet with the ETC team at the Sprint Planning Meeting.

An upcoming rollout TPB is described, and the Sprint is started. High-priority TPB items might have to be divided into segments so that they can be done within a single Sprint. All rollout Sprints start and end on the same day to synchronize the work involved.

A Sprint Review is held at the end of every Sprint. Tangible changes are demonstrated. Sometimes a rollout team might have nothing to demonstrate. This might mean that the wrong people were on the Sprint or they weren't spending enough time on the problem. Possibly, the problem was too difficult to solve as stated or in the current conditions. If this is the case, the ETC team should restructure the TPB, the rollout team, or both and then try again.

The Scrum adoption process is formally initiated with a Scrum kickoff meeting.

Scrum Kickoff Meeting

A kickoff meeting initiates the Scrum adoption and the ETC project that is responsible for its success. This meeting lasts three hours and is attended by the probable ETC team members, as defined earlier. An agenda for this meeting has the following items:

- **Review Scrum**   Ensure that everyone present understands Scrum.
- **Describe adoption process**   Management learns how ETC will work and how it will cause the Scrum adoption to occur.
- **Make decision**   Management at the meeting decides to proceed with Scrum.
- **Establish ETC Scrum team**   Formally define the ETC Scrum team composition, meeting times, and meeting places.
- **Kick off the first Scrum projects**   Identify the first Scrum projects for the rollout. They should be numerous, be across the enterprise, require rollout and integration, and place stress on the enterprise. They will start building product immediately while identifying impediments to product development.
- **Establish initial Transition Product Backlog items**   Identify the highest-priority work. These items usually include developing an enterprise Product Backlog, developing and implementing integration facilities, and selecting and training ScrumMasters.
- **Identify Scrum rollout teams**   Identify probable team members to be on the first Scrum rollout teams, and assign someone on the ETC team to notify them of their participation and the meeting schedules.
- **Schedule the first Sprint Planning Meeting**   Set a date to kick off the first Sprint with a Sprint Planning Meeting. Sooner is better than later.
- **Close the meeting**

A more detailed agenda for a kickoff meeting is shown in Appendix C, "Example Scrum Kickoff Meeting Agenda."

Chapter 3
The First Year

We've looked at why and how to adopt Scrum for your enterprise. This chapter lays out a probable timeline for the first year of the Scrum adoption. The first month will be the most hectic, and you'll feel a desire to wait until this is planned more thoroughly. Don't. The problems that erode productivity and effectiveness in your enterprise won't wait—they will continue to hurt. The adoption may not be perfect, but it is self-correcting. And, while it perfects itself, the problems are being addressed.

The First Month

The time has come to conduct the first ETC Sprint Planning Meeting. The time and date for this meeting were established at the Scrum kickoff meeting, described in Chapter 2, "Scrum qua Scrum." Since the kickoff meeting was held, members of the ETC team have formed Scrum rollout teams for the first Sprint. These teams and the full ETC team participate in the Sprint Planning Meeting.

The Transition Product Backlog (TPB) presented at the first Sprint Planning Meeting, which lists the first work to be done, will most likely consist of at least the following items:

- Communicate to everyone in the enterprise why Scrum is going to be used and how it will be rolled out. Communicate this often and in every way possible (handouts, company meetings, departmental meetings, and video conferences).

- Communicate how Scrum will affect the enterprise and the people within it.

- Provide Scrum training to everyone in the enterprise, and inform them the reason for the adoption, what is planned, and what is expected of them. Emphasize that Scrum is not a new methodology, but instead is a workout process to improve the enterprise.

- Provide a way for people to ask questions and resolve issues about Scrum and its impact on them.

- Establish preconditions that must be met before a project can use Scrum. These preconditions can be separated into minimum, median, and optimum phases so that projects can start prior to everything being in place. Create TPB items to fulfill these preconditions.

- Identify the first projects to use Scrum.

- Identify the Product Owner, ScrumMaster, and teams for these projects. (All projects start with one team.)

- Define Scrum metrics and the mechanisms for gathering and managing with them.

- Begin creating an enterprise Product Backlog.

- Identify likely ScrumMasters.

- Assess compensation policies to encourage teamwork.

- Define Scrum project reporting requirements.

- Establish a Scrum Center.

Some of these items are described in more detail in Appendix D, "Initial Enterprise Transition Product Backlog."

The Sprint Planning Meeting lasts less than one day. It will be over when, according to Scrum rules, the Scrum rollout teams have met with the ETC Product Owner, selected and committed to a backlog for the first Sprint, and figured out a plan (Sprint Backlog) for fulfilling their commitments. Figure 3-1 illustrates the Scrum implementation process.

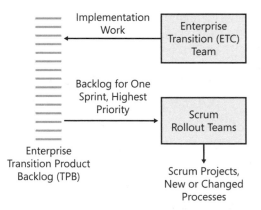

Scrum Implementation Project-ETC

Figure 3-1   Scrum adoption process diagram

The process shown in this figure will be used, Sprint after Sprint, to adopt Scrum throughout the enterprise. The TPB will grow as the work required to adopt Scrum becomes better known and as the impediments and changes are identified. Depending on the determination of the enterprise and the leadership from the ETC team, the adoption will occur more or less quickly, and more or less painfully. Scrum adoption is a project to change the enterprise's processes, the people who use the processes, and the culture that surrounds the processes.

An example of this is Ford Motor Company, which is attempting to change its process for scheduling car manufacturing. Leading the project is Mark Fields, who understands the difficulty of implementing change. Mark had a sign created and placed in Ford's Way Forward war room on which is written: "Culture eats strategy for breakfast."[1]

The adoption has started. The first rollout Sprints are underway.

The Second Month

By the start of the second month, many new Scrum development projects have been started. A deadly sin is to put off starting projects until they are perfectly staffed, formed, and planned and have a Product Backlog in place. Immediately start the first Sprint for the projects most important to the enterprise. Suddenly, product increments are being built by Scrum teams. At the same time, every reason that you had for not immediately starting the projects can be identified as an impediment. Put these impediments in the ETC Transition Product Backlog, and fix them. Meanwhile, the Scrum development teams are building software. Never wait for perfection; you can be adequate and still use Scrum. You won't necessarily have everything perfectly in place, but that's OK because you don't know what this journey consists of and where it will take you. But you'll be well armed because you are using Scrum to guide your journey.

The ScrumMaster is responsible for removing or fixing anything that makes his or her team less productive than it could be. Some of these things can be fixed by the ScrumMaster. But the ScrumMaster might not have the authority, knowledge, or scope to fix others. The ScrumMaster takes such problems to the ETC team's daily Scrum. There, the impediments are either quickly resolved or are put in the TPB for prioritization and later resolution. The unresolved impediments noted by the ScrumMaster are placed on the TPB along with those uncovered by the ETC team, as shown in Figure 3-2. While teams are using Scrum to build products, ETC is directing the work that will make them more productive.

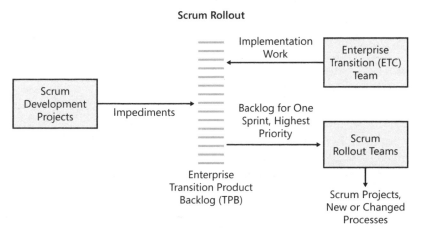

Figure 3-2   Scrum rollout

As the enterprise uses Scrum to build products, conflicts arise between current practices and the way Scrum works. Scrum is a highly optimized process for developing products, with a side benefit of making visible anything that gets in the way of doing so. Scrum exposes every dysfunction in the enterprise. Most of these are known and old culprits that have been tolerated. Now they are glaringly obvious and must be removed. These conflicts are put in the TPB.

The TPB frequently changes as new challenges and unexpected work are encountered. The ETC team continually reviews and reprioritizes the TPB to reflect these changes. It forms and reforms Scrum rollout teams every Sprint to do the next priority in the TPB—this is the process of adoption.

Sources of Transition Backlog Impediments

Many enterprises use the waterfall process to build products. In this process, requirements are thoroughly gathered at the start of the project. These requirements are progressively decomposed into architectures, designs, code, tested code, and documentation. Each part of the decomposition is done by experts in that function. The work of one function is communicated to another through documentation and artifacts. One would think that waterfall habits would be only in the development organization. However, waterfall habits form everywhere in an enterprise. Customers are accustomed to the waterfall approach of development. The human resources department is accustomed to setting up career paths and job descriptions that match waterfall processes. Finance is used to funding and monitoring waterfall projects. As you use Scrum, the differences between Scrum philosophies, practices, and habits and those of the waterfall approach will create conflict. The way people think about and do their work will have to change.

These impediments never stop arising. As top-priority impediments are fixed, new impediments become visible. As people come and go in the enterprise, new impediments arise. As market needs change or any other stress hits the enterprise, new impediments become visible and hurt productivity.

The following list describes some ways to identify impediments on an ongoing basis:

- **Brainstorming**   Get any group of people in a room. They can readily identify current problems. This is true for senior managers, middle managers, project managers, and developers. The things that are wrong prior to using Scrum will also be wrong when Scrum is used. The difference is that the wrong things will be more painful, difficult, and frequent because they run counter to Scrum practices. For instance, if there are more active projects than developers, it will be very difficult to form full-time Scrum teams. To solve this particular problem, start only Scrum projects to which people can be assigned full time.

- **Scrum Development Projects**   When a Scrum development project is underway, the team and Product Owner will run into impediments. These impediments are reported to the ScrumMaster at least as often as the daily Scrum planning session, the Daily Scrum. If the ScrumMaster or team can't resolve these problems on their own, they will be put in the TPB to be solved.

- **Conflict**   When Scrum projects get going, conflict occurs as people and organizations disagree on the best way to do their work. If not rapidly resolved, conflicts become conflagrations that destroy productivity. For instance, if an analyst is accustomed to always writing a specification and giving it to the programmer to code, this might no longer be needed or productive when they are members of the same team.

What If?

The Scrum adoption project, led by the ETC team, might encounter impediments in its operation and its Scrum rollout teams might fail to deliver committed changes. Sometimes this is because the rollout teams don't consist of the right people. In these cases, you should inspect team composition. Is there adequate authority and domain knowledge on the team? Do people know how to go about the work? Sometimes people on the Scrum rollout teams are delegating the work to subordinates or aren't participating at all. They feel that the change is then someone else's problem. However, the people on the Scrum rollout teams commit to making change. They are the ones who do the work to bring about the change, and they cannot delegate that work to anyone else or blame anyone else for the commitment not being met. If they aren't willing to do the work, they aren't the right people to have on the team. Remove them, and reformulate the team with the right people.

Maybe the change targeted by the Sprint is too big. If this is true, ask the rollout team to deconstruct the change into actionable pieces. Then have the team select a TPB item and initiate another Sprint.

Sometimes, there are too many important changes to be made. This is the same problem that many Product Owners have: too much work and too little capacity. Focus first on prioritization. Are the most important things being done first? Then focus on team composition. Is there a way to add productive people to these teams? Then focus on progress. Even though there are still many things to improve, look back and savor the changes already made. Then exercise patience and restraint. It took years to build these impediments, bad habits, and dysfunctions. It will certainly take years to remove them.

Regardless of which impediments you encounter, keep pressure on the rollout teams to deliver. Posting the TPB where it is visible to the entire enterprise helps. Under mounting pressure, teams will reorganize to become more productive.

The Third Month and Beyond

Take a step back and look at all the things that aren't going well; look at all the problems that you and your enterprise are struggling with. Separate these problems into two columns: problems that Scrum has brought in, and problems that always have been there and Scrum is highlighting. In most adoptions, the second column contains almost all the problems you are struggling with.

Scrum affords complete transparency. Everything is visible. You are made fully aware when the productivity, the progress toward goals, the competence of people to do their jobs, the willingness of people to work together toward enterprise or project goals, and the ability of engineering to build completed products on time is less than you desired or expected. Before you started adopting Scrum, you might have suspected what the problems were that undercut these intangible enterprise assets, but now it's obvious that these suspected problems are reducing your enterprise's ability to build and deploy competitive products.

At this point in the adoption cycle, many people in your enterprise are probably advising you to change Scrum because it needs some tweaking to be compatible with your enterprise. My advice is this: *Don't Do It.* The rules, roles, and time-boxes of Scrum are few and simple. The practices and structure of Scrum uncover problems that are sometimes ugly and difficult to solve. The normal tendency is to change the aspect of Scrum that made the problems visible. Everyone will then feel better and can proceed with their work just as they always have. Unfortunately, if you change Scrum, the very reason why their work is less productive than it could be will again be obscured. Whenever I visit an enterprise that is adopting Scrum, I look for these deviations from standard Scrum practices. In every instance, I have found an enterprise problem that everyone wanted to continue to ignore.

As changes are made by the ETC team, accommodations between old ways of doing business and the new might be sought. For instance, some parts of a project might still be using the waterfall process while other parts are using Scrum. However, care should be exercised to ensure these accommodations are temporary and don't become a permanent way of doing business.

Some enterprises have thought of modifying Scrum terminology to be more compatible with the enterprise's current practices. The hope is that the impact of the change can be softened. Unfortunately, what usually happens is that everyone in the enterprise sees this as a signal that the inclination to change isn't a serious one. For instance, if ScrumMasters are still referred to as a Project Managers, they will usually continue to believe that they are responsible for the success of the project and have authority to tell people what to do. The terminology of Scrum is abrasive to standard terminology and unusual so that everyone knows that a change is underway and that things are going to be different.

Some problems might require changing the way the enterprise does business. For instance, sales people might be accustomed to asking engineering people to whip up a quick prototype to help close a sale. This always seemed to work and not bother anyone. With Scrum, however, you can clearly see the impact of this approach on a project's progress at the Sprint Review. Because of the extra time and effort needed to fulfill off-the-cuff requests, the team probably won't finish everything that it committed to. You might have to come up with another mechanism for accommodating these sales requests. Now that you can quantify the cost to the enterprise of the interruption, you might even want the sales people to cost-justify prototypes in terms of costs, anticipated benefits, and probabilities.

Solving some of these problems requires more than one attempt. Scrum makes it obvious when a solution to a problem isn't perfect or when a problem changes and a solution needs to be rethought. Don't try for perfection in a solution; "good enough" is truly good enough to set the enterprise in the direction of perfection.

You and your management team will have to plot and scheme to come up with the best tactics. Exercises that help people understand the reasons for or benefits of a change to their daily work often help. Visiting other people or enterprises that have successfully adopted Scrum is often enlightening. You might need to devise and adopt metrics to encourage and track change. Be careful for unanticipated consequences these metrics might have on other areas, though. Your tactics will not always work. Expect that you will need to make many attempts. Expect that the solution might take some time to emerge.

The remainder of the book will provide you with some insights, tactics, and further information for adopting Scrum. As you have already realized, this adoption is really about optimizing your enterprise, and it will go on forever.

Chapter 4
Against Muscle Memory—The Friction of Change

If you find yourself saying that your group's developers have satisfied over 29 percent of their customers with successful projects,[1] they are probably relying on best practices, outstanding skills, cutting-edge quality, and a legacy of habits that form intellectual muscle memory. *Muscle memory* is a deep habit our muscles develop by working together. When the enterprise uses Scrum, the developer's muscle memory is inappropriate and damaging.

Expect muscle memory to exert itself. When a project is going well, everyone is happy with Scrum. However, when stress, a problem, or an unexpected failure occurs, everyone tends to throw away Scrum and revert to their muscle memory. Teams don't want to self-manage. They want to be told what to do. Managers don't want to let teams self-manage. They want to command the teams in all matters, down to the minutest detail. Teamwork is dumped for individual heroics. Quality is abandoned. Everyone draws on what they think has worked best in the past.

Four major muscle memories hinder Scrum's potential to effect change. They undercut the effort to build products better. Let's look at them.

Waterfall Thinking

The waterfall process emerged from project managers' wishes to overcome complexity with predictability. It has been the predominant development process used over the last 25 years. Waterfall is taught in universities, it's described in most process books and other literature as the correct approach, and the Project Management Institute has formalized it. Every project manager knows waterfall deep in his or her bones and feels it is correct. Habits accrued from waterfall development are embedded in enterprises. I call this "the tyranny of waterfall"; it is

---

1　Jim Johnson, *My Life Is Failure*, The Standish Group International, Inc., 2006, p. 2

inescapable. Even people who don't know it as the waterfall process think of it as the "right" way or "the way we've always done things."

When some people are asked to use Scrum, they are profoundly uncomfortable. It goes against the grain and feels risky. They reply, "Yes, but..." because their trained response is to prefer the waterfall practices. For instance, requirements are handled very differently with Scrum. About 50 percent of a typical project is spent developing requirements, architecture, and design. During the same project, 35 percent of the requirements change and over 65 percent of the functionality described by the requirements is never or rarely used. Regardless, in waterfall, all requirements, architecture, and infrastructure are fully detailed before the team builds functionality.

Scrum views requirements and architectures as inventory. Inventory is a liability because if some requirements change or aren't used, the time spent to understand them or design for them is a waste. The Product Backlog, which lists the requirements of Scrum, only has to be defined in time for a Sprint Planning Meeting; the work to fully understand it is performed only as the Sprint that transforms it into product occurs. Requirements are developed and architecture emerges in the Sprint for which the Product Owner requests them. To someone steeped in waterfall thinking, this practice is imprudent, risky, and reckless. To develop code from incomplete requirements, they know, is just asking for trouble. A waterfall architect told a Scrum architect that the only way to build a solid architecture was to think it through up front, before any code was built. The second architect said he thought that building it as requirements emerged might create a more stable architecture because it would be proven, piece by piece.

Let's look at the implications of another waterfall habit, functional specialization. The Product Owner discusses the Product Backlog with the Scrum team. Together, the team members discuss the requirements and create designs, code, tests, and documentation. A waterfall traditionalist believes, however, that only a designer can design, only a programmer can code, only a quality assurance (QA) person can test, and only a technical writer can write documentation!

I was attending a Sprint Review Meeting. The Scrum Team had selected five items from the Product Backlog for the Sprint. Only one item was finished. The team members said that the QA (testing) people on the team hadn't completed their testing. However, a Scrum team is cross-functional. The entire team is responsible for building completed pieces of functionality every Sprint. It wasn't the QA people who didn't finish the testing—the Scrum team didn't finish the testing. Scrum counts on everyone chipping in their best effort to do the work. When functional expertise is necessary, the people with those skills take the lead, but anyone can do the work.

Trey Research (TR), our first hypothetical company, develops acoustic products. TR was ready to introduce a new radio. Thousands were in the warehouse ready for shipment. Dr. Trey is the founder and CEO. As Dr. Trey read the user manual in his office, his frown got deeper and deeper. Finally, he called the technical writing manager, Matthias Berndt. Dr. Trey said he was very disappointed in the documentation; it was unusable. Berndt agreed, but said that it accurately reflected the way the radio worked. Dr. Trey kept his calm as he asked Berndt to go to the warehouse, open a radio box, and see if it worked the way the user documentation indicated. Two hours later, Berndt appeared in Dr. Trey's office with an open box and the user manual. Berndt said, "Much as I hate to say this, Dr. Trey, the manual accurately reflects the radio's operation."

Dr. Trey lost his temper. He asked Berndt how he could have let such a terrible radio be built. Didn't Berndt know that the radio was unacceptable? Berndt agreed, but he said that he had nothing to do with the radio until after it was built. Dr. Trey grew even more troubled and asked, "You mean, even though you've worked here 23 years and know our radios inside out, you don't have anything to do with their design? You only document them after they are built?" Berndt confirmed this. This dysfunctional approach was the impetus for TR to adopt Scrum. Now everyone on a cross-functional team at TR designs the radios. Dr. Trey knows that if the radio's design doesn't meet the approval of the engineers, technical writers, and testers, it shouldn't be built.

Command and Control

Workers are best able to figure out how to do their work, not their managers. The work is complex and has unexpected nuances. If workers are bound by someone else's instructions, they aren't free to do the work the best way possible.

Attendees at the Certified ScrumMaster class examine the productivity of self-management through an exercise. First, a contained space of approximately 400 square feet is established. Chairs, tables, and other obstacles are liberally sprinkled throughout the space. Everyone is placed in a pair, each pair consisting of a boss and a worker. The exercise is for the bosses to get their workers to take 60 full steps in two minutes using the commands of start, stop, left, right, faster, and slower. At the end of two minutes, about 50 percent have gone 60 paces. The rest have gone fewer paces. In the second part of the exercise, pairs are broken up. Everyone is a worker who manages his or her own activities. Each is free to use the previous commands or come up with more appropriate commands. Everyone is asked to take 60 full steps and then stop. Everyone is done within one minute. The self-management of the second exercise has doubled productivity. And because managers are now also workers, productivity has quadrupled.

Certified ScrumMasters know that self-managing Scrum teams are more productive. The front 10 percent of their mind is sold on self-management. But the back 90 percent knows that they are still in charge. If anything goes wrong, they will step in and tell the team what to do. We have been trained that this is the best way to absolutely make sure things go right. The command and control habit is very difficult to discard.

It takes time for Scrum teams to gel and start performing. Some teams require more support than others. The ScrumMaster is responsible for teaching self-managing teamwork to the team. For instance, if the team comes to the ScrumMaster saying, "This Product Backlog item is too large for one Sprint! What do we do?", it isn't told the answer. Instead, the ScrumMaster leads the team through the process of figuring out how to deconstruct the backlog. The ScrumMaster teaches; the team learns and finishes the exercise. The next time a similar situation arises, the team will know how to act independently. The moment the ScrumMaster tells the team what to do and how to do it, he or she exerts command and control. In command and control, the ScrumMaster believes he or she is responsible for productivity and problem solving. In self-management, the manager thinks that he or she is responsible for teaching the team self-management and problem solving.

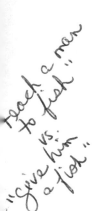

One project that I initiated included more than 50 developers. New development had to be done in conjunction with maintenance of the existing system. A reasonably good Product Backlog was in place. I spent several days reviewing employee files and resumes, as well as talking with the managers, trying to decide the best team composition. After those several days, I had a headache. So I called all the developers into the room. The Product Owner reviewed with the developers the upcoming project and the Product Backlog. I described the rules for composing Scrum teams and determining their size. We then asked the developers to organize themselves into teams. We told them the teams didn't have to be permanent but they should give it their best shot. Within four hours, they had formed their own teams. The teams created agreements among themselves about how the teams would cooperate. During the next Sprint, several team members shifted to other teams. At the end of that Sprint, the developers told us they were pretty happy with the team composition. They asked if they could continue to change as needed, however. We, of course, gave permission—we didn't have any better ideas!

Commitment to Defying the Laws of Nature

I live in Boston and frequently work in New York City. In just 45 minutes, the Delta Airlines shuttle can take me from Boston's Logan Airport to New York's LaGuardia Airport. I sometimes pack more than one meeting into a day because of this convenience.

One day, I was up first thing in the morning and down to New York for a meeting. I got back to LaGuardia by 2:00 P.M. to catch the 2:30 shuttle to Boston. I had an end-of-day meeting in downtown Boston at 4:30 P.M. This schedule would have worked, except LaGuardia was fogged in and all the afternoon flights were delayed or canceled. I went over to the Hertz counter. I told the Hertz clerk that I needed to be in Boston in 90 minutes and wanted a car. She looked at me strangely. Apparently, my need couldn't be met. The laws of the road, the top speed of the cars available, and the distance between Boston and New York City made my requirement pitiable and impossible to satisfy. The laws of physics thwarted my wishes.

Now consider a Product Owner at TailSpin (our next hypothetical company) who has met with her Scrum team prior to the first Sprint. She handed out a presentation with 12 bullet items. She told the team the 12 items had to be done and the release needed to ship within six months. The team looked blankly at the Product Owner and told her that, even without knowing more details about the project, it was impossible to do. The Product Owner answered, "If we don't deliver these features by then, we cannot sell the product, so it has to be done." Just like me in New York, this Product Owner needed something that wasn't possible.

Business runs on commitments. When you make a commitment to someone else, you have given your word. The other person arranges his business accordingly, counting on you to do what you say. This understanding is based on trust and is a tremendous source of efficiency. Let's give ourselves a short test on commitment. Read the following exercises and see if you can commit to fulfilling the other person's needs.

- Someone asks you to commit to having some item built for them. She asks you for the date on which it will be finished and for the price that it will cost. You spend some time with her trying to understand exactly what she wants, but the details are elusive. Also, you are going to have to handcraft this thing. You aren't sure of the exact skills of your workers or their availability. Also, the flu has been sweeping the town, and it could hit your team. The technology for building this item has worked so far, but a new release is coming out with mixed reviews. The person asking for the commitment also tells you that she might need to change some things along the way. Do you commit?

- Someone tells you that he wants a product by a specific date. You must do this thing because he has already committed the product by this date to somebody else. He wants you now to back up his commitment with your commitment. You aren't sure exactly what the whole commitment is, but the other person has power over your career and salary. Do you commit?

Of course, it is impossible to openly commit in either circumstance. You just don't know. You might feel that you have no choice but to commit in the second instance, but you had better have some tricks up your sleeve in case you get in trouble.

Pressuring someone to commit to an outcome regardless of what he or she believes is possible is a bad habit. If the person under pressure is honest, she won't promise anything. If she is cornered, she might make an undeliverable commitment. Neither alternative—a lack of commitment or a false commitment—is helpful if you need something to happen. Our muscle memory tells us that we can ask our engineering team for a commitment. The engineering team's muscle memory is to provide one, regardless of the circumstances. Where the waterfall process is in vogue, we have no choice but to do so. But we have other options when Scrum and iterative, incremental processes are used. These Scrum alternatives are presented in depth in Chapter 9, "The Relationship Between Product Management/Customer and the Development Team."

Hiding Reality

Our next hypothetical company is Coho, one of the largest resellers of cars in Europe. Senior management was rolling out Scrum to improve its ability to introduce new capabilities to customers. In the first Sprint of the first project, the Scrum teams delivered more functionality than they had committed to. Everyone, from senior management to the customers, was excited and pleased.

For the second Sprint, the Scrum teams committed to a large amount of Product Backlog. Two weeks into the Sprint, the teams realized they were in trouble. When the teams got together, they all had the same story: the functionality was significantly more complex and difficult than the first Sprint. Of the 24 pieces of functionality the teams had committed to, they figured that they might complete 7 or 8. After the way everyone had cheered them on at the first Sprint Review, they feared what would happen if only 33 percent of their second Sprint were done. The teams decided the only way they could deliver everything was to drop testing and refactoring; they would just slap the new functionality on top of the old. They figured that by committing to far less for the third Sprint they would have time to go back and fix it all.

One of their ScrumMasters asked them what they were doing. The ScrumMaster realized that Scrum is about empirical progress and transparency, so the Product Owner always knows what is going on and can make the best decisions. Wasn't the approach the team decided to take hiding things from the Product Owner? Weren't they pretending that things were done when they weren't? The teams, after expressing their fears that the Product Owner might fire all of them, went to the Product Owner and showed him where they were and what problems they were running into. The Product Owner looked at them and said, "I knew you overcommitted. I was going to ask you what was going on. I hoped maybe you knew something that I didn't. Well, I'm really glad you came to me." The Product Owner and teams reduced the commitments to match their new findings and proceeded, Sprint by Sprint, to build a great new system.

When I discuss this kind of fear at courses I teach, the attendees' own fear is palpable. The soon-to-be Scrum users don't think that transparency, or truth, is acceptable where they work. They tell me that they will be fired if they tell the truth. Truth isn't what their customers want to hear. They tell me their customers will find someone else who will lie to them if they don't. I have seen this in class after class for five years. People in product development think that their customers want to hear news only if it is good news and would rather hear a lie than the truth. "Lying" is a harsh word. But what else do you call saying that something is true when you know it not to be true? What else do you call misleading someone with information or holding back information that would have led them to better decisions? The Product Owners want to believe in magic, and the developers support the belief by lying. "Can you do this project by this date?" "Sure, no problem."

The developers are aware of the complexities that cause changes to their original estimates. They are aware that the customer is unhappy. If a project manager is approached by a customer 60 percent of the way through a project and asked how the project is going, the project manager doesn't really know. She knows that some things are going well. She also knows that some things are not going so well. She also knows that she hasn't checked up on some things that could prove critical. However, saying "I don't know" is unacceptable, so project managers have learned to say, "Right on," "Right on target," "Piece of cake," or anything equivalent that will get the customer to go away and leave them to try to get everything on time, on cost. Basically, they lie. It is simpler than exposing all the nuances and complexities that add up to "I don't know."

Project managers might also believe that lying saves time. But because Scrum relies on transparency, misrepresentation undercuts the entire application of Scrum. If the Product Owners do not know exactly where things stand at any point in time, they will be unable to make the best decisions possible about how to achieve their goals. They need the best information possible, whether they view it as good or bad.

Summary

The iterative, incremental nature of Scrum causes change within the enterprise. The enterprise must adapt to monthly project changes, not just change at the very end. A project produces potentially usable increments of the whole system every month. Teams produce complete pieces of that increment daily. This frequency of completed work causes change.

Dysfunctional behavior that was hidden becomes visible. Problems caused by the dysfunctional behavior are magnified. As you solve the dysfunctional behavior, don't think that the solution is complete. For 25 years, every habit described in this chapter has provided better solutions to people in your enterprise than anything else has. Now these people are going to try something better, something that even feels right. But when the problems of product development and management arise, your people are going to feel naked. They haven't accrued muscle memory in these new ways yet. So, because it feels safe—just for now—they return to these habits, the old-reliable habits. Your enterprise and its people will take four steps forward, three steps back, two steps forward, one step back. They will continually progress, but they will bemoan their inability to ignore and transcend old habits. Scrum, however, won't them let ignore the consequences of these habits.

Chapter 5
Enterprises in Transition

Enterprises that see value in Scrum decide to move forward. This chapter presents cases of companies that have moved forward with Scrum. (I have changed the real names of the companies and people involved to fictitious names.) These were courageous enterprises, motivated by insight and need. No enterprise in its right mind would wholeheartedly start using Scrum otherwise. Adopting Scrum in an enterprise is like looking into the abyss, girding oneself for an epic journey, and then making the plunge. What will be discovered and have to be conquered is different in each enterprise; what is common is the courage to start and then persist. Most enterprises that have a compelling need to change take the easy way out—they hire management consultants, buy another business to distract themselves, or reorganize. Scrum is soul-searching by examining failures and dysfunctions, not based on philosophical whim. It is a perilous journey, but probably the only one worth making, because it is the serious business of self-improvement. It is taking a hard look in the mirror every day, every month, and doing something about what one sees.

Every enterprise that uses Scrum plots a different course. The people are different. The problems are different. The urgency of the problems is different. The only commonality is Scrum as a tool for change. We'll look at enterprises I've had experience with to illustrate some lessons that can help your enterprise effectively implement Scrum. In all of these examples, the companies saw value first and then plunged into Scrum adoption.

Contoso

Contoso builds value-added card products, such as gift cards issued in various dollar amounts. Customers include retailers, banks, insurance companies, and malls. It has a sophisticated core system, featuring a value-added card template that lets customers define the specific features of their value-added card. The developers at Contoso customize the template to uniquely brand and sell the cards to consumers. Contoso's ability in the past to rapidly create sophisticated products had made it a marketplace leader. For instance, if your company wanted to sell someone a value-added card that let them buy only certain products made by specific manufacturers during a certain date range, Contoso could easily handle this. The value-added product would be specified, and a fixed-price, fixed-date contract would be signed between your company and Contoso. The project to develop it would typically last four or so months. Contoso's business model is to at least break even on these projects. The profit is generated by the transaction fees collected when consumers start using the value-added cards.

Situation

Contoso customers were angry. A significant number of projects to build customized value-added cards were late or didn't deliver exactly what the customer wanted. The project team would look at the specifications in the contract, work with the account manager for that customer, and develop what it thought was correct. The newer contracts had some sophisticated features requiring changes in the core product, which often took longer than the contract allowed. Everyone worked a lot of overtime, over and over, to minimize the damage. However, the damage was accumulating. An increasing number of customers were unhappy. Staff turnover at Contoso was nearing 50 percent per year. An employee survey of the development organization indicated that only 15 percent of employees were pleased to be working there.

New challenges arose. Existing customers envisioned more products for the upcoming holiday season; they insisted on putting severe penalties for late delivery into the contracts because these products were useless if delivered after the holidays. A further challenge was that success with one value card in one marketplace caused everyone else to want to provide a card with even more sophisticated functionality. Contoso was overwhelmed. The number of new contracts far exceeded its capacity to deliver. Contoso's development organization couldn't keep up. Contoso's success was in danger of unraveling. Competition arose as Contoso struggled to meet its commitments.

Experienced developers were burnt out and leaving. Contoso couldn't hire and train new developers fast enough to meet the demand. Contoso investigated the possibility of using offshore development organizations to add just-in-time capacity. The vision was to train key people in an offshore company, and they would then train the rest of their organization. As volume rose, the offshore organization would supply more and more people until demand was met. It was a perfect solution—extensible resources on demand. Except, it didn't work. The offshore companies took too long to come together, and it was difficult to synchronize changes to core functionality. Even more chaos and dissatisfaction ensued.

Application of Scrum

Senior management at Contoso had read several papers about Scrum and were hopeful that it would help. Their back was against the wall, and they were ready to try anything. As they said, it couldn't get any worse.

Contoso had a mature process improvement organization. It had previously performed a value-chain study, which is a Lean Thinking[1] practice that identifies wasteful practices, on the customer change request process. Over 30 steps for handling any change request were identified. They simplified the process to five steps.

In an appalling move contrary to everything that I've ever said, Contoso adopted Scrum whole hog. Within two weeks, the process improvement organization had converted all existing work to Scrum. It formed new Scrum teams, appointed ScrumMasters, and found Product Owners. It gave overview courses. There were 29 new Scrum teams, 29 new ScrumMasters, and 29 new Product Owners.

The process improvement organization was a top-down, command and control, metrics-driven group. It implemented metrics to monitor the progress of Scrum projects. The VP of the process organization met daily with all senior management to review impediments, progress on contracts, and trends in the metrics. Problems were really, really transparent. Fixes were rapidly devised and deployed. Plus, productivity more than doubled within the first three months of adopting Scrum.

Outcome

An employee survey after just two months of using Scrum showed over 85 percent of the employees pleased to be working at Contoso. Employees were even recruiting their friends. More products were being completed on time with the functionality the customer needed. Many customers were shifting from punishing fixed-price, fixed-date contracts to short, two-page time and material contracts. The customers felt so in control of the product development and the risks involved that they trusted their ability to stay in charge of the development. The customers would "hire" a team for six months to build the product they envisioned. If the team got done earlier, the customer would have the team return for the next product. One customer had a fixed-price, fixed-date contract that called for delivery within six months. When Contoso delivered in six months, the customer wasn't ready for the product. The customer had hedged its bets, assuming that Contoso would probably be late.

Additional Comments

Contoso became the marketplace leader for value-added cards, outperforming all its competitors. Its accomplishments attracted the attention of a much larger financial products company, TailSpin. TailSpin saw two opportunities. Contoso would fit nicely into its portfolio. Also, TailSpin was having increasing trouble building its own products. Its management hoped to learn from Contoso expertise.

---

1 James P. Womack and Daniel T. Jones, *Lean Thinking* (Free Press, 2003)

Contoso was a piece of coal that became a gem, and it was then was acquired by TailSpin and turned into coal dust. TailSpin thought of people as resources to solve problems rather than people to be enabled. Because TailSpin viewed its employees as plug-and-play components, the company tried mixing in cheaper offshore "resources" on projects. Productivity was cut in half, quality dropped, and communications with the offshore vendors went bad. Customers went from joyously managing time and material contracts to again demanding fixed-price, fixed-date contracts.

In one telling episode, TailSpin misinterpreted the idea of collocated team space. TailSpin thought collocation was to save money, so it collocated the entire development organization in one room. Desks were pushed next to each other in rows until over 200 developers were crammed into one room. The developers called this a Scrumeteria, since it reminded them of a high-school cafeteria.

People make Scrum work. They are presented with problems, they make commitments, and they creatively excel in solving the problems. Scrum happens bottom-up. But if top management doesn't understand and lead, the enterprise will not be able to sustain the productivity and creativity provided by its employees.

Humongous

Humongous is one of the nation's largest bank-based financial services companies, with assets of approximately $96 billion. It provides retail and commercial banking, consumer finance, and investment banking products and services to individuals and companies.

Situation

Humongous' Information Technology (IT) organization consists of over 1,000 people with a new development budget of over $100 million. The development organization had trouble reliably delivering systems that satisfied its internal customers. As a remedy, the Senior VP of development acquired and rolled out a major, modern methodology, Really Improved Process (RIP). Its rollout was planned and executed by the Software Development Support Center within two years. Unfortunately, nothing improved and the internal customers remained unhappy. As a next step, the Senior VP met weekly with each project manager in his conference room to review key project metrics. Project managers realized that any slips could result in career damage.

The Senior VP was replaced by Mark Bebbington, a seasoned professional who had successfully used Scrum on many critical projects. He summed up the situation by noting that the users hated IT. Users had turned to buying packages. Mark decided that Scrum was appropriate at Humongous. Scrum's philosophy of personal accountability and empowerment with creativity were needed.

Application of Scrum, Phase 1

Mark didn't "roll out" or "implement" Scrum. He understood that it isn't a methodology. People have to want to use it for their projects to be successful. Mark decided that he would use the "osmosis" approach. He focused only on projects where both the user and the project team wanted to use Scrum. Their successes would become visible and others would follow. Mark provided Scrum training to his management and to project managers and users who expressed interest. He also trained the Software Development Support Center so that it could support any project that decided to use Scrum.

At the same time, Mark decided to make Humongous a more hospitable place for software development. He started removing any outstanding problems or impediments. He initiated a transition Scrum. His management listed and prioritized the major problems with software development at Humongous. This list became the transition Product Backlog, with Mark as the Product Owner. He then started Sprints, staffed by his entire management team, to remove these impediments. As impediments were identified in Scrum projects, they were added to the Product Backlog. Creating these transition Scrum teams became on ongoing process.

Mark also set preconditions for any project that wanted to use Scrum. For instance, a project had to have a full-time staff, a committed Product Owner, and a willingness to use collocated space. When a project met these criteria, the Software Development Support Center trained and supported it.

Outcome, Phase 1

After 18 months, several critical projects were vividly successful using Scrum. A new system for all Humongous tellers had even been presented to the Board of Directors. It was an impressive model of development and user collaboration.

However, Scrum's roots weren't very deep at Humongous. The skill level of most developers was low with regard to Scrum. Although the developers were using the vocabulary, many thought that attending a Daily Scrum was what Scrum was all about. Then they would tell others that they were "Scrumming." Many customers hadn't bought into Scrum. They still liked giving their requirements to development and not having any more responsibility for the project. IT management also largely hadn't bought into Scrum. They mouthed the words and said the right things. But they continued to behave as they always had. To paraphrase their attitude, "I really know how to manage, and I'm going to stick with what has worked before."

Despite top executive support within the IT organization and a fertile environment, Scrum had not become the normal way for software to be developed within the company. Most employees were still comfortable with their jobs and the way things had always been done. They saw Scrum as something that would pass, just like all the other novel approaches seen over the years. However, whenever a customer had a critical project, the customer was demanding that the Humongous development teams use Scrum. These projects set a benchmark within the user community for anyone who had an urgent request and cared to devote time to it.

Situation, Phase 2

In this phase, Mark now has some capital to work with. Some users are extremely pleased with IT. The attitude of the Board of Directors has become positive. Some developers are very productive and work to make their users happy with the best solutions possible. Everyone knows Scrum, and the vocabulary is widely used. The question Mark now faced is how to use this capital of goodwill to expand the beachhead.

Application of Scrum, Phase 2

Mark decided to shift from osmosis absorption of Scrum to something more dramatic and visible. Mark's organization supports five major groups within the bank. Henrik Jensen is the head of one of these groups, consumer banking. He decided that he had enough evidence to require all his people to use Scrum. Mark talked with the head of Henrik's IT group. He agreed to go from cosmetic change to real change using Scrum to do all of Henrik's projects.

To make this change happen, Mark and Henrik got everyone together and set the ground rules. Everyone was expected to use Scrum fully, and overall results were expected to improve. The Software Development Support Center would now focus all of its support, training, consulting, and coaching to projects in this one group. All projects would be subjected to "Scrum audits" by the Software Development Support Center to determine correct Scrum usage.

The Software Development Support Center pulled together metrics to include "smells" that are intangible, but telling. For instance, if a team isn't collaborating during the Daily Scrum and the project can't be clearly understood by an outsider, self-management isn't occurring. If the team and the Product Owner aren't collaborating during the Sprint Review, the Scrum steps of inspection and adaptation aren't occurring. If the Product Owner is surprised during the Sprint Review, he or she isn't working closely enough with the team. If an up-to-date Product Backlog burn-down chart and Product Backlog isn't posted at the Sprint Review, the Product Owner isn't managing the project. The Software Development Support Center decided that the primary metric it would measure would be surprises. Any surprises would be indicators of incorrect use.

Outcome, Phase 2

Mark and Henrik have changed their organizations, and progress is being made. After the consumer banking division begins its adoption of Scrum, the enterprise will have another group starting down the right path.

Additional Comments

Scrum helped Humongous achieve some critical successes and avoid some potentially devastating failures. The entire enterprise became more competitive and profitable as a result of using Scrum. However, it isn't nearly as competitive and profitable as it could be. Projects still waste time writing requirements documents. They are far less productive than possible. They are producing lower quality functionality than desirable. However, the beachhead is in place, and a better way to build software is evident to both developers and users. The leaders now must continue to lead.

Woodgrove Bank

Woodgrove Bank is a very large, innovative financial services company. By parsing credit profiles and closely assessing risks, Woodgrove Bank has extended credit to market segments largely ignored by its competition. By offering flexible credit products with rewards, Woodgrove Bank has built one of the largest card-holder bases and card assets in the world. By dynamically tracking the profile of each of its customers, the bank provides services that maximize revenues. For instance, if you call support for any reason and your last payment has been no more than three days late and your overdue amount is less than 10 percent of the total due, a 30-day high-interest deferral plan is offered to you.

Over the last seven years, Woodgrove Bank's ability to create innovative functionality in its credit products has slowed. At first, it seemed to just take longer than usual to add some new features. Eventually, new features started breaking other parts of the credit card system that had previously worked. The relationship between IT and the business degraded as IT was unable to deliver what was needed on time. Maintenance grew to consume over 40 percent of all development costs.

Woodgrove Bank's credit card processing was its best money-maker. The profits were incredible. Unfortunately, other financial institutions noticed this. They started emulating the credit card products that previously had been Woodgrove Bank's undisputed domain. Worse, the other financial institutions were now able to add more features to their credit cards faster than Woodgrove Bank could.

Three years ago, Woodgrove Bank decided that it had to rewrite its core credit card processing application to be more stable and amenable to new functionality. The Mobius Project, a 30-month project to rebuild core credit card processing capability, was initiated under a waterfall process. This was a very complex effort, and the compressed project schedule didn't help the process.

During this project, the competition kept eating away at Woodgrove Bank's market share. The developers were pressured to get the project done. The new system was tremendously important. Woodgrove Bank successfully transitioned to the new credit card processing system in 2006, having successfully survived Mobius's tight project schedule and a high-risk implementation strategy.

Application of Scrum

In 2004, the CIO set a goal of cutting time-to-market in half by the end of 2005. As part of that effort, the CTO and a small group of internal consultants looked into Scrum as a way to help solve this problem. Several projects were started using Scrum, and the value was obvious to the entire enterprise.

In 2005, more difficult projects were piloted using Scrum. They were still screened, though, and selected only if they looked like good fits. They were stacked with top-notch employees to see whether Scrum projects would work under ideal conditions. As these projects succeeded, larger and more complex projects were piloted with continued success. An Agile Center of Excellence was formed. Program offices run by Scrum champions began the process of organizational change. One group started seven teams concurrently on the same platforms and had great success. Throughout the year, training staff in Scrum and selling the idea to the rest of Woodgrove Bank continued. To ramp up more quickly, outside consultants were relied on to help Woodgrove Bank avoid pitfalls.

In 2006, the CIO set a goal to have more than 50 percent of the entire IT portfolio delivered using Scrum. This goal was successfully met by the third quarter. An underlying goal was to cement Scrum as a way of thinking and conducting business. To make Scrum part of the culture, the CIO conducted frequent open space meetings and regular informational meetings. Top-notch trainers were contracted to get projects going and to mentor the team members throughout. Scrum was used on all types of projects from very large, complex, and interrelated work to entire pipelines of enhancements and defect fixes.

Best of all, the relationship between internal customers and IT was significantly repaired. The motivation for using Scrum shifted from stopping the bleeding to leveraging it to create competitive advantage for Woodgrove Bank. Scrum was coupled with Lean Thinking techniques to create a weapon used when competing with the very large competitors in Woodgrove Bank's space. One of the biggest areas of growth for Scrum was in work outside of IT. Operations, marketing, compliance, and many other teams began leveraging what IT learned by adopting Scrum for all complex projects. Even advertising campaigns used Scrum.

Woodgrove Bank also made the transition away from relying on external consultants and experts. The bank began using internal consultants and ScrumMasters to support new teams. Woodgrove Bank now employs a formal mentoring program, where experienced coaches work with new ScrumMasters. Certified coaches are also plugged into the community to encourage continued learning and growth. The mentoring program and focus on community has enabled Woodgrove Bank to rapidly scale its use of Scrum while maintaining the level of quality in the teams. Regular community events are used to share experiences and keep everyone on the same page.

Lean Thinking and Scrum are being partnered as Woodgrove Bank goes forward. Lean Thinking value stream mapping is used proactively to identify areas of waste that can be removed. Scrum is used to manage the projects as well as empirically identify further areas of waste and other impediments.

Litware

Litware is a typical independent software vendor (ISV). It has been selling products to software developers for over 20 years. Its revenues are around $100 million per year. Litware releases new versions of its products annually. Product marketing prepares a marketing requirements document that carefully itemizes all new functionality and requirements. These are prioritized as "must have," "should have," and "nice to have." The program management office prepares a detailed plan that, when followed, results in an appropriate new release. The creation and validation of this plan requires two to three months to complete. Then work starts.

Situation

Release 3.51 was typical. The 120 developers began analyzing the requirements document and designing the new release. At the same time, though, new requirements began to appear. The plan was updated.

By the fifth month, everyone was getting a familiar sinking feeling. There was too much work left to meet the scheduled release date. The developers started simplifying the design. By the seventh month, as more changes kept arriving, the developers started to work long hours and weekends. Everyone was feeling pressured and worried. To increase productivity, the developers also stopped redesigning the code to handle new functionality. They instead "plastered" new code on top of existing code. Unit testing disappeared along with code and design reviews. "Alpha release" was shortened to one week to fit in some last-minute functionality. The developers didn't have time to fix all the reported bugs.

In the end, release 3.51 was three weeks late. It didn't contain all the last-minute requirements and was of marginal quality. Nevertheless, the developers were proud that they had moved it out the door. They could now start to lead a normal life, see their families, and fix some of the most egregious bugs.

On the Monday following the release, Litware's CEO called for a meeting with everyone in the development group. He surprised everyone by telling them that they were *not* getting a bonus this year. They were flabbergasted. They had worked their hearts out and forgone a normal family life for at least four months! But the CEO reminded them that the release had been late and didn't have everything that had been asked for. Already the customers were complaining about the poor quality. The CEO then paused, looked at the haggard developers and said, "By the way, you look pretty bad. Maybe you should take better care of your health."

Application of Scrum

The development group at Litware selected Scrum for its practice of sustainable pace. They reasoned that if they weren't going to get a bonus, at least they wouldn't be worn out after the next release! No enterprise had ever selected Scrum for such an unflattering reason. The VP of Development, Stan Hatz, had no problem selling Scrum to the CEO and management.

Everyone had been so dissatisfied with the process for release 3.51 that they said, "It couldn't get any worse!"

I worked closely with Stan throughout the Scrum implementation at Litware. There were days when Stan and I despaired of ever undertaking the project. Every problem that had been ignored to date suddenly was visible, big, and ugly. Stan could continue forward only when he looked back at the progress already made. We also noticed that every problem we encountered had been at Litware long before Scrum was known. When we implemented Scrum, however, they became evident. For example, the development group at Litware had previously struggled to get a release shipped by the scheduled date. Scrum demanded that they have a full increment every Sprint. Everything that had made this difficult to do yearly was now difficult monthly.

At the end of just one Sprint, however, the developers were able to show management functionality that was potentially shippable. Everyone wanted to build on this success, so their willingness to work through the problems increased. Problems were seen in terms of their impact on this monthly progress, rather than as isolated events that could be ignored. For instance, if the daily build of software wasn't successful, other daily builds might not be successful. And by the end of the Sprint, nothing might be available for viewing and shipping. The feedback was immediate, and the consequences were tangible and near-term.

Outcome

As Litware's management watched release 4.1 emerge, Sprint by Sprint, they saw an opportunity. The user conference was coming up. The user conference was a great social event, but it hadn't been very useful for real product information because no real product was available. Usually, marketing would present screen mock-ups and prototypes of what the upcoming release might look like. This time they had a partially developed product actually working, and the functionality was of the highest value to the customers and prospects. Why not show them the actual product? A contingent from the development enterprise was invited to demonstrate the partial release at the user conference.

The customers were ecstatic. They were thrilled to be asked their opinion based on real functionality. The developers were delighted to collaborate with marketing and customers about what to do next. The entire experience was extremely gratifying and reinforcing for everyone involved.

At the user conference, one of Litware's largest customers, Woodgrove Bank, had been impressed by some of the functionality in release 4.1. The Litware salesman handling the bank's account, Danny Forte, reported to the VP of Sales, that Woodgrove Bank wanted to buy more copies of Litware's new release 4.1 if Litware would just add a couple of additional pieces of functionality. Then Woodgrove Bank would be willing to license an additional $14 million dollars worth of product.

Fourteen million dollars isn't much money to huge enterprises, but the opportunity to add it to the $100 million annual revenue at Litware was very compelling. It was so compelling that the Vice President of Sales talked to the CEO, who told Stan to make it happen. Stan then told the developers, "Make it happen, no matter what." In the software industry, this means to build the additional functionality into the product and keep the same date. Just do it.

Three weeks before the scheduled release date, I visited Litware to check up on its progress. When I got off the elevator at the development floor, I knew something was wrong. There was no noise. A characteristic of an enterprise using Scrum is community, people working together on ideas, collaborating over different approaches, sharing in work. No noise was not good noise.

In the work areas, the team members all had their heads down at their workstations, looking grim. There was no joy, no excitement, no sharing. I gathered a group of the developers and asked what was going on. They replied that the overtime was killing them. I asked how this could be since Scrum called for a sustainable pace. They told me that the additional $14 million dollars from Woodgrove Bank would make the financial year. Without the new functionality for Woodgrove Bank, the target release date was December 1. With the new functionality, the release date should have changed to January 15, but it had been ordered to be done by the target date. Stan had told them to do whatever it takes.

Development velocity is a measure of the developer's ability to turn requirements into shippable functionality across time. A significant increase in development velocity was required to build this new Woodgrove Bank functionality by the initial release date. Velocity increases are gradual, the result of better development tools and practices, and of better teamwork. How could the velocity have increased so quickly? The developers told me what I suspected. They increased their velocity by working nights and weekends and reducing the amount of work by cutting quality.

I became irritated. I asked the developers how this was different from release 3.51, when they were exhausted, the product was shabby, and the dates and functionality were missed. Had they forgotten? The developers said that they hadn't forgotten, but Stan had told them to do it, so they had no choice.

I knew Stan well by this time and was surprised. When I went to see him, he was stunned. He hit his forehead with his hand and said, "I absolutely forgot! When the CEO and VP of Sales came to me, I knew that we needed to do it for the business, so I reverted to old form. My old habits took over, and I did what I used to do. Now we are building this release with poor quality and exhausted developers just like before."

Stan decided to get the developers back on the track to building a quality product at a sustainable pace. Because the sale to Woodgrove Bank was critical, he asked the developers to include it as quality functionality! We then calculated the new delivery date for release 4.1.

It was eight weeks after the initially planned date, including time to restore lost quality and build the new functionality.

Stan called the CEO to confirm the new schedule. Adding $14 million dollars to that year's revenues was attractive, but was the cost of the eight-week delay acceptable? A meeting was set up for the next day with the CEO, the VP of Sales, the VP of Marketing, and the Chief Financial Officer (CFO). In the meantime, Stan and I calculated the cost of the release's delay. Including additional development costs, delayed maintenance revenues, and several customers that we might lose, the probable cost was $5 million dollars.

At the meeting, the VP of Sales started by saying, "I may not be a PhD in Mathematics, but $14 million dollars looks at lot larger than $5 million dollars. Let's do it! Right, Danny?" He looked over at the Woodgrove salesman. But, Danny wasn't meeting his eyes. When a salesman doesn't meet your eyes, it is a very bad sign. So, he again asked, "Right, Danny?" Danny looked up and said, "Well, I don't actually have a signed contract yet."

The VP of Sales at that point asked to reconvene the meeting the next day. When we got back together, Danny wasn't with us. (He was no longer with Litware.) It turned out that he not only didn't have a contract, the person he had been dealing with didn't have the authority to sign a contract. Worse, the budgeting period when funding could occur was six months later! Danny was behind in sales for the quarter and had been overeager at the user conference. He had detected a Woodgrove Bank manager's interest in release 4.1. The manager had indicated that he wanted some more functionality. Danny had figured that if he could get it, he would then have a lever to get the manager to sign for more products. The $14 million dollars was simply a projection based on a hypothesis to support Danny's need to hit sales targets.

Why not? To Danny and the VP of Sales, it cost nothing to demand the functionality. They never saw the direct correlation between these demands and the product quality, which got worse release by release. They never correlated these demands with the turnover and generally poor morale in the development enterprise. They figured that the development enterprise always had slack. They always had been able to fit more into a release in the past. So why not ask for more again?

Additional Comments

Two major changes occurred from using Scrum, both causing ripple effects far beyond their immediate point of impact. First, customers and prospects were able to see release 4.1 early and evaluate major pieces of it. They responded to this change enthusiastically, thinking of additional uses for the product within their enterprises.

Second, the sales force saw the customers and prospects responding differently. They saw sales opportunities because excited customers could mean additional sales. When more sales revenues were seen as possible, everyone reverted to form and fell back on the habits of release 3.51 and before. Management told the developers to do what it takes to build more functionality within the same time period. Consequently, the quality of the product and staff suffered. Only when reminded of their "muscle-memory" behavior did they rationally evaluate the reality of the opportunity.

Increments of software were produced every month, and the customers were able to see them at the user conference. What could be better? But every change has two sides, and we tend to focus on the good side. The opportunity provided to Danny was one of the unanticipated, negative consequences. In our haste and eagerness to only see the good, we sometimes miss or ignore the negative parts of change.

Part II
Start Using Scrum for Enterprise Work

New processes and practices are demanded as your enterprise removes dysfunctions and problems identified with Scrum. When Scrum is used in a single project, these changes are isolated. When the enterprise adopts Scrum, these changes are widespread. Section 2 lays out some processes, practices, and techniques that will help you adopt Scrum at an enterprise level. None of them are new. They are just different from the way work is currently done. The types of practices described are noted in the following list of chapters in this section:

- Chapter 6, "Organizational Practices," covers practices for organizing the work of the enterprise.

- Chapter 7, "Engineering Practices," addresses integrating enterprise work regardless of the technologies, architectures, or processes used.

- Chapter 8, "People Practices," describes what changes are needed for people to successfully use Scrum in self-managing, cross-functional teams.

- Chapter 9, "The Relationship Between Product Management/Customer and the Development Team," looks at the new relationship that is formed between Product Owners and development teams. This is the mother of all changes. If it doesn't succeed, you don't accrue Scrum's benefits.

Several caveats apply to these changes. This section consists of proven practices and processes. You probably will have to refine them for your enterprise. Let the people who are going to do the work define and refine the new practice or process. If you define it for them, they will feel that they can't continually modify them to meet new circumstances. Second, don't plan a perfect process or practice. Just come up with one that seems appropriate. Any shortcomings will immediately be detected by Scrum. You can then refine it. Enterprises often try to get it perfect before starting. During this time, they could have been building product.

Chapter 6
Organizational Practices

When your enterprise uses Scrum, you can monitor all development every Sprint. You can redirect enterprise work to take advantage of new opportunities and maximize enterprise return on investment (ROI). The entire enterprise can change course quickly. To be able to do these things, you must have all your enterprise's work in a single Product Backlog. Creating such a backlog can take over one year and is very difficult. Once it's done, however, you'll wonder how you managed previously. Without an integrated picture of all of the enterprise's work, it is impossible to assess progress and perform impact analyses.

In this chapter, I'll explain how to create such an enterprise Product Backlog. An overview is presented in the "#1: Organizing Enterprise Work" section. The enterprise Product Backlog structure is somewhat different for high-technology product enterprises than it is for an enterprise that deploys technology to make its operations more competitive. We'll look at high-technology Product Backlogs in the "#2: Organizing Enterprise Work for a High-Technology Product Company" section. In "#3: Organizing Enterprise Work in Other Enterprises," we'll look at creating a Product Backlog for other enterprises.

Another Product Backlog variant is organizing work when a new enterprise operation, including systems that automate it, is being developed. This scenario is discussed in "#4: Organizing Enterprise Work for New Systems that Automate an Enterprise Operation."

A Product Backlog is the work of the company. Many views of this work are often required. The "#5: Organizing the Complexity of Multiple Views" section shows how to correlate and manage multiple views. The information in this section will help you handle some complexities of maintaining multiple views.

Finally, we'll look at how to organize work if your enterprise is using a software product family architecture to optimize reusability in "#6: Organizing Work to Optimize Software Product Family Architectures."

#1: Organizing Enterprise Work

Scrum seems to organize work into Product Backlogs. But how do I organize my entire enterprise's work into a Product Backlog and what are the benefits of doing so?

We can organize all of an enterprise's development work into an enterprise Product Backlog. To create an enterprise Product Backlog, create an enterprise view of all projects and programs. These views are top-down decompositions that organize the Product Backlog by enterprise product architecture, organization, or programs. If the enterprise sells high-technology products, use a product decomposition that consists of the following information: product family, product, features, function, and task. If the enterprise uses technology to automate its products, like a financial institution does, use details of the organizational structure. The rest of this chapter presents ways of creating these views and linking them to each project's Product Backlog. As we correlate and link the detailed Product Backlog of Scrum projects to the enterprise view, the enterprise Product Backlog starts taking form. We then fill in the enterprise Product Backlog as more projects are started. You must eventually identify, organize, and prioritize all current and planned work.

To the degree that all the work of the enterprise is in an enterprise Product Backlog, you can track the progress of every program, release, and project through burn-down charts. For any area of interest, a burn-down chart tracks progress toward a release goal across time. With burn-down charts, you can assess the impact various projects and programs have on each other and on the enterprise. You probably will be unpleasantly surprised. Programs that you thought were well underway might be behind. You might find that splitting people across many projects has slowed overall work rather than allowing the enterprise to take on more. You will get a lot of information, some confirming your hopes and others dashing them. You will, however, have solid information with which to manage the enterprise.

#2: Organizing Enterprise Work for a High-Technology Product Company

My enterprise builds products that we sell to external customers. Scrum organizes work into Product Backlogs. How do I organize my enterprise's work? In particular, if I have an opportunity to do something new, how do I quickly reorganize to do so?

A Product Backlog can represent all known development work for an enterprise's products. The products decompose into features, functions, activities, and tasks, reflecting the product structure and terminology. A Product Backlog defines the changes that are needed at this lowest level. This decomposition can be aggregated into product families and all of the enterprises' development work, as shown in Figure 6-1.

Product Family	Product	Feature	Function	Activity	Backlog	ID
Personal Finances	......					
Corporate Taxes	......					
Personal Taxes	WhirlWind Deluxe	Personal Information	About You			
				Filing Status		
				Personal Information		
				Location		
				Mailing Address/Phone	User must be able to type in different format telephone numbers	C413
				State of Residence		

Figure 6-1   Enterprise Product Backlog

A product or system architecture consists of modules or components at the lowest level of decomposition. One or more of these components will be changed to satisfy a Product Backlog item. We can organize a separate Product Backlog for product functionality common to more than one product. This Product Backlog's structure reflects the system's architecture, as shown in Figure 6.2. Overall prioritization for the good of the enterprise is mandatory. The Product Owner of the common functionality has to be someone with return on investment (ROI) responsibility for all enterprise products.

Aspect	Activity	Task	Module	ID	SPF Prty	SPF Size	CI Prty	CI Size
Screen User Interface	Controls	Formatted Numeric Entry	Domestic Telephone Number	C413	72	2	61	1
Business Logic								
Data Base Controls								
Data Base								

Figure 6-2   Common infrastructure Product Backlog of requirements

Let's look at how we could respond to a customer requiring enhanced functionality in the Corporate Taxes product family. We estimated the effort to make the enhancement at

100 points of work. (A point of work is an arbitrary measure.) The customer needs it within six months. We are in the fifth month of our enterprise's annual plan.

An enterprise burn-down chart shows the annual baseline plan, as shown in Figure 6-3.

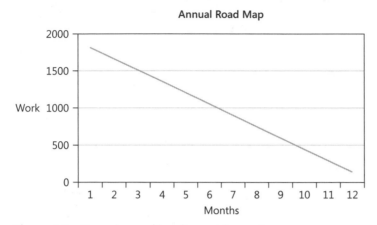

Figure 6-3   Burn-down of baseline roadmap plan

We assess progress against the plan. The plan is maintained in an enterprise Product Backlog. The measurement is against the most current plan, which is usually different from the baseline plan. In the fifth month, we can compare the currently planned functionality against that which has already been delivered, as shown in Figure 6-4.

The difference between the two plans represents the degree to which the enterprise is ahead of or behind plan. Figure 6-4 shows that we are behind our plan and behind on our commitments.

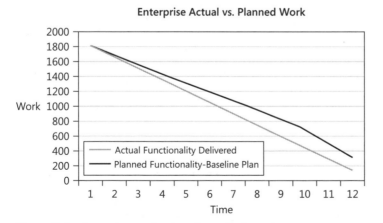

Figure 6-4   Burn-down of enterprise actual vs. plan

At the end of the fifth month, the plan committed us to have 1214 points of work left. Instead, there are 1320 points of work left to be completed. If we add the new 100 points of work requested in the Corporate Taxes product line, the planned versus actual measurement becomes worse, as shown in Figure 6-5.

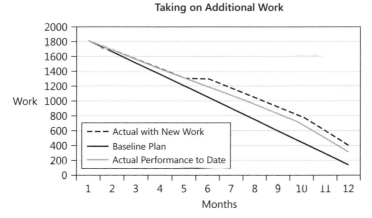

Figure 6-5   Burn-down of actual vs. plan with new work added

The planned work is the bottom trend line. The actual work left without the additional work taken into account is the middle trend line. The top trend line shows actual work remaining if the new work is committed to. All of these trend lines have been projected to year end to show the probable gap between planned and actual work.

To take on the additional Corporate Taxes enhancements, we need to decommit to other work. We could increase costs through additional new hires, but productivity drops as new people are brought on board and increases only after six or so months. We need to find some other work that we can defer. First, let's add the new work to the Corporate Taxes part of the Product Backlog. It is the fifth row of Figure 6-6. We then estimate and prioritize it compared to all other work in the enterprise's Product Backlog. For Scrum estimation techniques, see Mike Cohn's recent book, *Agile Estimating and Planning* (Prentice Hall, 2004). The prioritized enterprise Product Backlog (summarized) looks like Figure 6-6.

We need to accommodate 206 new points of work (100 new points of work added to the current shortfall of 106 points). We can decommit lower priority work. The first item to put on hold is the lowest priority in the bottom row: Personal Taxes, State of Residence, Item 6. The remaining 148 points of work to be deferred (206 needed less the 58 points of Item 6) has to come from the Personal Finances product, the next lowest priority. Its entire workload has 1048 points of work planned for the year.

Enterprise	Product Family	Product	Feature	Function	Activity	Backlog	ID	Domain	Prty	Size
	Personal Taxes	WhirlWind Deluxe	Personal Information	About You	State of Residence	Item 5			90	33
	Personal Taxes	WhirlWind Deluxe	Personal Information	About You	Mailing Address/Phone	Item 3			82	47
	Personal Taxes	WhirlWind Deluxe	Personal Information	About You	Mailing Address/Phone	Item 4			73	33
	Corporate Taxes					New work			72	100
	Personal Taxes	WhirlWind Deluxe	Personal Information	About You	State of Residence	Item 7			65	29
	Personal Taxes	WhirlWind Deluxe	Personal Information	About You	Mailing Address/Phone	Item 2			63	52
	Personal Taxes	WhirlWind Deluxe	Personal Information	About You	Mailing Address/Phone	User must be able to type in different format telephone numbers	C413	Common	62	20
	Corporate Taxes					Committed work			42	432
	Personal Taxes	WhirlWind Deluxe	Personal Information	About You	State of Residence	Item 8			21	82
	Personal Finances					Committed work			12	1048
	Personal Taxes	WhirlWind Deluxe	Personal Information	About You	State of Residence	Item 6			11	58

Figure 6-6 Enterprise Product Backlog with new work

When we drill down and look at the burn-down for the Personal Finances product line, it is ahead of plan. We then drill down into its work to see where we can free up some effort while minimizing the impact. In Figure 6-7, we drill down to look at just the work for Personal Finances.

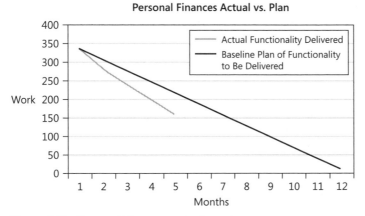

Figure 6-7 Personal Finances actual vs. plan

The Personal Finances work is ahead of schedule. At the end of the fifth month, we had planned to have 217 points of work left, but only 160 remain. We are 57 points ahead of plan. We might be able to use this capacity for the new work in the Corporate Taxes product line.

Drilling down in the Personal Finances work, we can see which specific areas are ahead of plan. Then we can assess whether the people doing that work are skilled and capable of helping the Corporate Taxes product. If they are, we might be able to redeploy them. We will ask the Product Owner of the Personal Finances product line whether he or she can form a new team that can be reassigned for four months.

This exercise took care of the new work and enabled us to get the new customer's business. We assessed the enterprise's ongoing work to identify excess capacity. We could do the same thing every month to detect shortfalls and slippages.

As priorities change and new opportunities occur, we can realign our work to maximize enterprise ROI. The Product Owners at every level of the enterprise are able to track their work against their commitments. We can shift the enterprise to take advantage of new opportunities while assessing and then tracking the impact.

#3: Organizing Enterprise Work in Other Enterprises

My company uses our Information Technology organization to develop software for my line operations. This software makes the operations more effective. How does the management of these operations use Scrum, or do I leave this to the Information Technology department?

Product Owners are the managers of their operations. They define work to enhance their products in the Product Backlog. The development work can be to enhance automated systems or manual operations. Training and implementation work is also part of the Product Backlog. The Product Backlog is sorted by System and Priority to organize work within the Information Technology (IT) organization. IT teams are formed based on Product and System identifiers.

We can use the following example of a banking enterprise to see how to do this. A bank sells financial products to its customers. It is organized into lines of business (LOB). Each line of business consists of operations that sell and service financial products. These operations are automated through internal systems. For instance, a bank can have a Trust LOB, a Commercial Banking LOB, and a Consumer Banking LOB. Within the Consumer Banking LOB is a Teller operation, a Loan Creation operation, and so on. These are serviced by a Product Development and Management department that devises the various financial products. Each operation is supported by one or more computer systems. As new products are conceived, the operations and systems supporting them must be developed or enhanced. The Product

Backlog, or requirements, to do so are organized by LOB, operation, activity, and task. Figure 6-8 represents such a decomposition.

Enterprise	Line of Business	Operation	Product	Activity	System	Component	Requirement	Prty	Size
Bank	Trust	......							
	Corporate Banking	......							
	Consumer Banking	Teller	Mortgage						
			Savings	Deposits	Teller31	C524	Customer can make a deposit across accounts	33	13
						C325	Customer can perform deposit themselves using new automated teller terminal	42	21
				Withdrawals					
			Checking						
		Platform	IRA	Filing Status					
			401K	Personal Information					
			Mortgage	Location					
			Personal Loan						
			Savings						
			Checking						

Figure 6-8   Financial enterprise Product Backlog

#4: Organizing Enterprise Work for New Systems that Automate an Enterprise Operation

We are building a new system for a division in our enterprise. It will replace a patchwork, older system. How can the work be directed by the Chief Operations Officer of that division so that it makes sense to her, while being organized and prioritized in a way that makes sense from a systems architecture viewpoint?

Data is the business of some enterprises, such as credit reporting, encyclopedias, news, and mapping. These enterprises acquire, format, and sell data. Enterprises sometimes need to build entirely new systems for these type of operations. The managers of these operations need to correlate and prioritize developing a new business operation with building new systems to automate it.

The business operation is organized into several primary functions. The data is acquired. The data is continually groomed to provide additional value through new relationships and attributes. The data is managed for accuracy and quality. The data is extracted for sale to customers. Some extracts are periodic, while others are continuous. At the lowest level of the business operation, activities and tasks are performed. These tasks are manual, manual with automated assist, or completely automated. The automated system is organized as an architecture that has nonfunctional attributes such as performance, scalability, security, and workflow.

The person who runs this operation is the Product Owner. He or she is responsible for overall profitability and the long-term investment in the new system. He or she is responsible for prioritizing the development to support a phased, secure implementation as well as for meeting technical dependencies. As an example of technical dependencies, the workflow framework might be essential to have in place prior to implementing acquisition and editing functionality. The intersection of operational and systems decomposition is shown in Figure 6-9. The Product Backlog work occurs at the intersection.

Divisions	Departments	Sections	Subsection	Activities	Tasks	Product Backlog	Component	Module	Subsystem	System
Operations	Acquisition									TCX01
	Grooming									TCZ01
	Data Management									TDX01
	Data Management	Security							TDX01-01	TDX01
	Data Management	Quality & Integrity Control							TDX01-02	TDX01
	Data Management	Quality & Integrity Control	New Data	Referential Integrity					TDX01-03	TDX01
	Data Management	Quality & Integrity Control	New Data	Referential Integrity						
	Data Management	Quality & Integrity Control	New Data	Referential Integrity						
	Data Management	Quality & Integrity Control	New Data	Referential Integrity	Set up Area		CSetup02	ReflInteg	TDX01-04	TDX01
	Data Management	Quality & Integrity Control	New Data	Referential Integrity	Select Area		CSetup03	ReflInteg	TDX01-05	TDX01
	Data Management	Quality & Integrity Control	New Data	Referential Integrity	Select Area	Display areas to be selected	CSetup04	ReflInteg	TDX01-05	TDX01
	Data Management	Quality & Integrity Control	New Data	Referential Integrity	Select Area	Display tables and indices for selected area	CSetup05	ReflInteg	TDX01-05	TDX01
	Data Management	Quality & Integrity Control	New Data	Referential Integrity	Initiate Check		CSetup04	ReflInteg	TDX01-06	TDX01
	Data Management	Quality & Integrity Control	New Data	Domain Integrity						TDX01
	Extraction									

Figure 6-9   Intersection of operational and system views in a Product Backlog

The Product Backlog item "Display areas to be selected" is part of the operation's Data Management function. It is used by the supervisor of the Referential Integrity section to frequently inspect and check data referential integrity. The new system has a component, CSetup04 (which is part of Subsystem TDX01-05 and System TDX01), to automate this.

The operational viewpoint also uses Product Backlog items to describe work to enhance a work activity, including creating documentation and retraining. It includes columns that reflect operational implementation priorities and efforts. The systems view includes a column for the effort to build the component and the priority in which it will be developed. The systems view also includes Product Backlog items for systems that provide infrastructure used by the other systems, such as workflow. Other work, such as constructing distributed development environments and upgrading the production environment, have their own Product Backlog items. This Product Backlog is prioritized according to the most logical sequence for developing the system.

#5: Organizing the Complexity of Multiple Views

I've seen how to create several views of an enterprise Product Backlog. But there are some complexities you haven't discussed. Can you describe how to handle them?

Product Backlog is a prioritized list of work. We can relate it to three areas: its occurrence in a product or system, its occurrence in improving a business operation, and its occurrence in systems architecture. We can then create complex views by intersecting these relationships. Figure 6-9, seen in the previous section, shows an example of several views of a Product Backlog. It shows the relationship of a business operational view (Divisions, Departments, Sections, Subsection, Activities, and Tasks columns) to the work in a Product Backlog (Product Backlog column), which is then related to the systems architecture view (System, Subsystem, Module, and Component columns).

Product Backlog items range from small to big. Small items usually relate to fine-grained business operations, system architectural components, or product tasks, as shown in Figure 6-9 earlier. As the items increase in size, the corresponding items they relate to increase in size. For instance, a Product Backlog item referred to as "Automatically flow applications from investigation to acceptance and notification" relates to subsystems, business activities, and product themes. It is large and high level.

Modules or components are often used by more than one operational task or product activity. The Product Backlog item to change a component then has to be entered one time for each time it automates the task or activity. However, it is estimated for only one of the occurrences. All occurrences inherit the highest priority need and are scheduled accordingly. Sometimes multiple occurrences of a Product Backlog item are indicated in one column in the spreadsheet.

#6: Organizing Work to Optimize Software Product Family Architectures

Some enterprises develop products and families of products. Some of the functionality is product specific, but other parts are shared among all products. How is this work organized with Scrum?

Many enterprises have more than one product. They often separate common functionality into a component infrastructure library to simplify defining new products or enhancing an existing product. When products are developed, some components are unique to the product, but other components might already be in the infrastructure, reducing overall development time and costs. If some potentially common functionality isn't already in the infrastructure, it is developed there to reduce the costs for future products. By keeping the infrastructure in good shape and well cataloged, new product development is simplified.

The role of the Product Backlog needs to be extended to address this common infrastructure. The Product Backlog usually just lists requirements of work to be done for a product. Now the Product Backlog will reflect the structure of the entire product family. The product family decomposes into products, features, functions, and activities, as shown in Figure 6-10. When something new is needed, the requirement is added. Some Product Backlog requirements will be satisfied by components or databases in the common infrastructure. Figure 6-10 demonstrates this by using the "Common" designator in the Domain column. If this is an existing component that needs enhancing, the ID for the existing component is recorded. When the Product Backlog is sorted by requirement priority and requirement, it starts with a prioritized list of work to be done.

The common infrastructure supports all products. It has its own Product Backlog. This is organized by aspect. This backlog is populated with maintenance work and all work requested for each Product Family and Product, as shown in Figure 6-11.

Product	Feature	Function	Activity	Backlog	ID	Domain	Prty	Size
WhirlWind Special	Personal Information	About You						
			Filing Status					
			Personal Information					
			Location					
			Mailing Address/Phone	User must be able to type in different format telephone numbers	C413	Common	72	2
			State of Residence					
			Multiple Residence					
			Other State Income					
			Occupation					
			Phone Listing Option	User must be able to type in different format telephone numbers	C413	Common	72	2
			Create User ID					
			Hurricane Katrina					
			Special Situations					
		Dependents	Dependents					
		Import Information	Import from Last Year					
		Dependents						
		Import Your Information						
	Federal Taxes	Income	Wages and Salary					

Figure 6-10   Software product family Product Backlog of requirements

Aspect	Activity	Task	Module	ID	SPF Prty	SPF Size	CI Prty	CI Size
Screen User Interface	Controls	Formatted Numeric Entry	Domestic Telephone Number	C413	72	2	61	1
Business Logic								
Data Base Controls								
Data Base								

Figure 6-11   Common infrastructure Product Backlog of requirements

The Product Owner for all product families prioritizes the infrastructure Product Backlog. Only this person can evaluate all product family priorities against each other and against the need to maintain and sustain the common infrastructure. This priority is maintained in the Common Infrastructure (CI) Prty column. The relative size of the work, as evaluated by the infrastructure teams, is maintained in the CI Size column. This work might be different in size than that estimated by the Product Team. Note that the duplicate Product Backlog requirements from Figure 6-11 have been merged into one.

Chapter 7
Engineering Practices

Development work happens in individual Scrum teams. These teams are often part of a larger project. Only when their work is integrated with that of other teams is it of use to the enterprise. To track the impact of individual teams on a project, you must integrate work frequently. Practices for doing so are presented in this chapter.

Scrum requires that all work be integrated at least once per Sprint. To accomplish this, teams usually must integrate their work with other teams at least daily, and preferably continuously. Frequently, integrating each team's work is difficult and your engineering organization probably can't do it, yet. To integrate each team's work, you have to change the way development is organized. You have to change the technology that you use to test and build products. Your organization's overall engineering skills have to improve. When these requirements were discussed in one enterprise I had worked with, the group manager told his management team that he wanted this done within two months. This demand led to a lively conversation about how hard this change was going to be.

Some of these changes are local to the developer and his or her Scrum team. However, most enterprises need significant, sustained improvements throughout. Products are complicated, despite the best architectures. You have to be tough-minded to build increments of these products frequently. You have to be merciless to know where the development stands every day. Engineering organizations frequently tell me what they can't do within Scrum: "We can't regression test everything within the Sprint window!!" and so forth. That is the wrong answer. The right answer is, "We can't do that now. We'll figure out how to do it."

Let's look at solutions to the engineering problem of frequently integrating work. I'll use examples from my experiences in the field, again substituting fictitious company names for the real ones.

#1: Multilayer System Work Organized by Functionality

How do we organize to develop an enhancement that includes new front-end functionality and enhanced back-end infrastructure functionality?

A company called Wingtip develops and markets Internet infrastructure software. Wingtip adopted Scrum in mid-2005. Within six months, all of its development projects used Scrum. Teams were organized to own specific functionality. Every team was instructed to select work for a Sprint only if it could completely test it, design it properly, and complete the user documentation. This was Wingtip's definition of a "done" increment, which was deployed monthly.

As part of a new release of Wingtip's advertising product, customer reporting functionality was going to be enhanced by the advertising development team. The team selected a Product Backlog item to allow a customer to display all ad types over a variable time period on one screen. Customers currently had to scroll among multiple screens and manually tally the counts. The work consisted of changes to the user screens, business logic, and database.

The ad server had most of the business logic and all the databases. It was part of Wingtip's infrastructure that supported all Wingtip's products. Existing ad server capability retrieved usage by hour and day for each usage type. To support enhanced reporting, the infrastructure had to be enhanced to maintain more time frames of usage. It also had to be able to aggregate counts for multiple ad types, which required additional database fields. Once the infrastructure was so enhanced, the front end could make a single request across the Internet with the variable for that account, time period, and ad types.

The infrastructure team was a separate team that maintained and enhanced only the infrastructure. There were only eight people who could do this in all of Wingtip, and they were on this team. This constrained other teams because nobody else was allowed to work on the infrastructure. The advertising development team told the ScrumMaster that it needed people from the infrastructure team. Unfortunately, the people they needed were booked for months. The team had to proceed without them with a localized solution that didn't require any infrastructure changes, as shown in Figure 7-1.

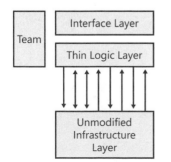

Figure 7-1 Localized solution

At the Sprint Review, the advertising team demonstrated the screen. The functionality was very slow. Because the infrastructure couldn't be changed yet, multiple requests were made to the infrastructure ad server for data, which the front end then accumulated. The advertising team mimicked the ad server in the front end.

The advertising team had developed the following localized solution:

```
Set up variables with account number and time period.
Set up a variable with all known ad types.
Pull the first ad type from a string of all ad types.
Request the count for that ad type, account, and day.
Aggregate the count in a counter.
Continue making requests across the Internet until the string with ad types is depleted.
Continue making requests across the Internet to the ad server until the time period is fulfilled.
```

Although this functionality worked, the team had devised a local solution that was far too slow to ship. The Product Owner asked the ScrumMaster to figure out how to get the needed help from the infrastructure team. The ScrumMaster devised the following enterprise solution. Teams could only build an increment that encompassed all necessary layers, including the infrastructure. If infrastructure support wasn't available, the team had to do other Product Backlog items first.

Another field was added to each team's Product Backlog to indicate dependencies on the infrastructure layer. In the following example, the use of "Infrastruct" in the Domain column indicates this dependency:

Feature	Function	Activity	Backlog	ID	Domain	Prty
Administer	Monthly Billing	Display ad counts	Allow a customer to display all ad types over a variable time period for his or her account on one screen	C213	Infrastruct	22

The work the infrastructure team had to do was added to the infrastructure Product Backlog, as shown in the next table. Other work was prioritized to be done before the ad server team's work.

Aspect	Activity	Module	Backlog	Source ID	Prty	Size
Advertising	Reporting	Ad aggregation	Allow a customer to display all ad types over a variable time period for his or her account on one screen	C213	42	8

A functional team and the infrastructure team would try to synchronize their work to the same Sprint, when they could work together, as shown in Figure 7-2. If the infrastructure team got the work done in an earlier Sprint, the functional team could make commitments to the overall functionality. Otherwise, the functional team had to defer its dependent work. It had to wait until the other team was available.

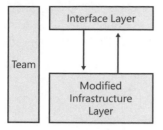

Figure 7-2   Enterprise solution—Teams build functionality across all required layers

Prior to the team selecting the "Display ad counts" Product Backlog item, the advertising team talked to the Product Owner for the infrastructure team. The people it needed were unavailable for the next two Sprints. The advertising team had to select lower priority Product Backlog for these Sprints. When the infrastructure people were available in the third Sprint, all layers—including infrastructure—were modified to provide a completely usable piece of functionality.

When the team completed the aggregation functionality, its localized code looked like the following:

```
Set up variable with account number, time period, and "all types" indicator
Request count from ad server
```

This solution required only two transmissions across the Internet, and it had adequate performance. One transmission made the request, and the other received the results. All the logic for determining what data was required, retrieving the data, and then aggregating it was placed at the ad server.

A Scrum technique for handling external dependencies arose from this situation. Whenever a team cannot do an increment because they have an external dependency, they cannot commit unless—and only unless—the other people or teams are also at the Sprint Planning Meeting. These external teams or people have to commit also. Otherwise, the external parties might be interested parties, but they certainly are not committed parties.

When an infrastructure team provides functionality for multiple products, who prioritizes its work? Each product's Product Owner will, of course, lobby for the urgency of his or her work. One solution is to integrate all the Product Backlogs into an enterprise Product Backlog. The burn-down and progress for each individual product can be tracked. The burn-down and progress for a family of products that is dependent on shared functionality can also be tracked. A Product Owner who is responsible for overall profitability prioritizes the infrastructure Product Backlog to maximize enterprise profits and reduce risks.

#2: Integration of Multiple-Layer Systems

How does an enterprise organize its work when it is developing an overall product with many functions and features but the work is divided according to the various architectural layers of the product?

Many products are architected into layers. Even a simple Web application has interface, logic, and persistence layers. In our example, Wingtip tied their layers together with teams that developed functionality across all layers. Sometimes this doesn't work and other approaches are devised. When devising these, keep in mind that any approach has to meet at least two criteria. First, we have to know where we are in a project at any time. Second, we have to be able to release a completed increment as often as possible.

Fabrikam produces an Internet-enabled alternative to cable and satellite TV. Fabrikam markets its products to telephone companies with large-scale DSL offerings. Fabrikam delivers its functionality through five layers. The first layer collects and stores all entertainment material. A second layer maintains customers and account information. These layers are located in common Fabrikam server facilities. The third layer packs, transmits, and unpacks entertainment from the Internet. The next layers are on the TV-top control box. The fourth layer manages programming and storage of entertainment. The fifth layer is for selecting and playing programs. Each of the layers was developed by separate organizations at different geographic locations: one layer in Israel, another in the UK, two layers at different locations in the United States, and one layer in China. Each layer had its own Product Owner and Scrum teams. The product and its layers are shown in Figure 7-3.

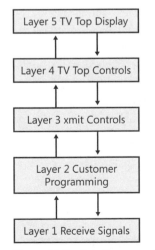

Figure 7-3 Fabrikam product layers

The fifth-layer team presented its progress at its Sprint Review in California. The team showed excellent progress in developing functionality on its layer. Not only was the functionality powerful, but its arrangement was elegant and intuitive. The other layer teams also presented their layers at their respective locations. They were all progressing according to the schedule. The Fabrikam Vice President was pleased with the progress.

After the Sprint Reviews, the ScrumMasters for all the layers had a conference call with me. They asked if, within the rules of Scrum, they could discontinue the *Scrum of Scrums*. They felt that the meetings weren't fruitful. They felt that very little information was shared that everyone was interested in. The geographical dispersion and time differences made these meetings even less worthwhile. Scrum of Scrums are short, daily Scrum meetings at which an engineer from each team working on an integrated product gather to share the status of their teams. This meeting helps teams keep track of progress between parts of the product so that they can more closely monitor any dependency or timing problems. I wondered why this wasn't important to the teams building the various parts of the Fabrikam products. Didn't they need to know each other's progress? When queried, the ScrumMaster for the fifth layer said that the progress of other layers wasn't important to his team. His team's Product Backlog and Sprint Reviews were only for his layer. I asked how his teams knew if its increment integrated with the other layers. He replied that they had very detailed specifications that they were developing to.

The interface design for each layer had changed since the project began. Unfortunately, teams at each layer were still building to the original and now out-of-date interface specification. Each layer was progressing, but nobody knew whether their increments integrated to form a complete product. Such a check would have exposed any integration discrepancies and allowed for corrective work. The participants in the daily Scrum of Scrums should have been tracking any changes from the original specification.

The Product Backlog is often decomposed by layers: architectural, functional, and geographical—or a mix of all of these. There has to be an overall Product Owner. He or she can delegate decomposed Product Backlog management to other Product Owners. In large projects, there might be four or five layers of Product Backlog decomposition. Each has a Product Owner reporting to the overall Product Owner. At any time, the combined Product Backlog dynamically describes the progress in developing a complete product.

The Fabrikam Product Backlog was combined into one Product Backlog, structured into the five layers. The Vice President became the overall Product Owner. By tracking the combined burn-down and trend lines, he could manage overall product development. However, as things currently stood, the various layers were unlikely to work together. The Vice President asked for a solution so that he could view an integrated, potentially shippable product as frequently as possible.

The teams at each layer built their own layer at least daily to see whether it still fit and worked together with other layers. The top engineers of the various levels met and reasoned that an integration of builds from all the layers could solve the problem. Overall product integration could then be checked and tested. This integration of efforts is shown in Figure 7-4.

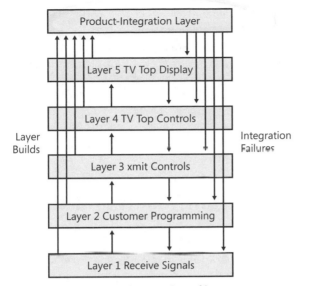

Figure 7-4   Frequent integration of layers

They took the following steps:

- They agreed to have a sixth level, an integration layer. The integration layer team was made up of people from each of the five other layers.

- The integration team implemented integration hardware and software. It pulled the builds from each layer daily and tried to integrate them into a single build.

- The integration team developed tests that ran through all layers and tested the integrated functionality. The tests exercised the layers as they would be operated when an end user tried to operate the TV.

- Integration failures were reported to the team working on the layer that had caused the failure. This team had to resolve the problem before moving forward with any more development.

- A rule was instituted that all five layers had to work as an integrated product at the end of each Sprint. If they didn't, none of the layers was done or could be demonstrated.

The work was added to the overall Product Backlog. It took two Sprints before an integrated product could be demonstrated. Incompatibilities and divergences from product specifications were exposed and had to be fixed.

Scrum's inspect and adapt techniques require a full, integrated increment. If the increment being inspected isn't complete, the adaptations might well be wrong. At Fabrikam, Scrum pointed out nobody was tracking the overall product development. The integration deficiencies wouldn't have been apparent otherwise until near the end of the project.

When products consist of more than five layers, integration is more difficult and takes longer. If the product consisted of features whose development cycles varied, the integration also might have been harder. For instance, hardware's build cycle is usually several months. If the hardware for Fabrikam's TV-top control unit was part of the development, another integration technique would have been needed.

The Wingtip example mentioned earlier provides insights into how to organize work in an enterprise for feature-driven development. Fabrikam provides insights into how to organize work within an enterprise for architectural-layer-driven development. These are only two of the many possibilities.

#3: Integrating the Work of Scrum Teams and Teams Not Using Scrum

A product is being developed by many teams. Some teams use Scrum. Other teams use a waterfall process. Other teams are developing hardware and use a proprietary process. How can all these teams be managed, and how can the Scrum teams fit their work in?

Trey Research develops audio products. A project was started to build a new radio. A Product Requirements Document (PRD) and plan were developed. Of the many teams formed, one hardware team and one embedded software team were responsible for building the handheld remote controller (remote). The hardware requirements were specified. The hardware would be a per-unit cost for every unit shipped. The cost of the software was a one-time cost. Accordingly, the hardware capability was minimized to save money. Commodity hardware was selected.

The hardware team was using its own milestone-driven process as it worked from the PRD. The milestones were a design document, a hardware breadbox, a prototype, and then the finished product. The breadbox was a large-scale, crude imitation of the remote controller. The breadbox contained buttons and controls that would generate the types of interrupts that the remote could expect and should handle. It provided a test environment for the embedded software and could be used to verify every Sprint's increment of functionality. However, the breadbox delivery milestone was three months into the project.

The software team used Scrum. The Product Owner and the team extracted the Product Backlog from the PRD that addressed software functionality. During the first three months, the software team completed three Sprints. It built a simulation layer to the specifications of the remote on a PC. Once the breadbox was delivered, development done on the PC would be tested on the breadbox.

In the fifth month of development, a competitor introduced a radio with more remote functionality than the Trey Research remote. In response, the goals for the Trey Research remote were expanded. The Product Manager rewrote the PRD and briefed both the hardware and software teams. She then worked with the software team to update its Product Backlog.

The hardware team figured to have a new design specification done in two months. A bread-box would be ready in three months. The prototype would be ready within six months. Until the new design specification was available, the software team couldn't detail the functionality of the simulation layer on the PC. The software team also wasn't sure whether all the new capabilities could be handled on the selected commodity hardware.

The more complex the product is, the more change and miscommunication can be expected. Scrum's answer is to require integration of all product components as frequently as possible, minimizing later rework. Integration should occur at least once per Sprint, and the integrated product is demonstrated at the Sprint Review. Sometimes other teams aren't using Scrum. Then the Scrum teams are required to integrate as often as possible to the best possible representations of the other parts of the system. These representations can be simulation layers, which are built by Scrum teams using the best available designs from the other, non-Scrum teams. Whatever is possible must be devised and used to minimize later rework.

Until the breadbox was ready, the software team had to build a simulation of the remote's new functionality and interrupt structure as best as it understood it. The team's starting point was the PRD and the Product Owner. The software team selected several enhanced functions and several new functions for the first Sprint. It refactored the design to broadly take the anticipated changes into account. It also ensured that the previously developed functionality continued to work.

By the end of the first month, the hardware team had partial specifications ready. For the second Sprint, the software team selected some more new Product Backlog. The team also selected several previously "done" items from the first Sprint. In the second Sprint, it expanded and refactored previous work to the new design information. It made detailed changes to the simulation layer. It then tested the previous "done" items to ensure they still worked. By the end of the second month, the hardware team had the design specifications done. During the third Sprint, the software team first rebuilt the simulation layer to reflect the new design. It then completely refactored and redeveloped previously done work to the new design. The software team tested it against the simulation layer.

At the end of the third month, the breadbox was done and delivered to the software team. If this were a perfect world, the breadbox and simulation layer on the PC would operate identically. To see whether this was true, the team and Product Owner placed the following new items on the Product Backlog for the fourth Sprint:

- Test functionality that worked on the simulation layer to see whether it also works on the breadbox. Rectify any discrepancies between the environments to the correct design. Correct the functionality if needed.

- Work with the engineering team to resolve overall discrepancies between the design and breadbox.

- Update the simulation layer accordingly.

- Continue to develop functionality for the rest of the Product Backlog.

During the fourth month, the hardware team was busy building the prototype. The software team continued Sprinting, but discovered that the commodity hardware was no longer adequate. The CPU was too slow and the memory too limited. The software team negotiated with the Product Owner and the hardware team to procure new hardware. This introduced new work for the hardware team. It had to revise the design, the breadbox, and the prototype. Completed work had to be revised to take into account the changed hardware performance and characteristics.

The software team revised the Product Backlog. It now had to simulate the new memory and CPU capabilities on the PC. It had to retest all completed functionality in this environment. The design documents were revised, and the breadbox with the more capable hardware was rebuilt. All completed work again had to be retested.

The solution just described required the software team to retest its work against the best possible representation of the completed product. Every time the design changed, these representations had to be changed for retesting. The rework was limited to that functionality and the design completed when the change occurred.

If the entire product was software, several teams could be developing functionality using Scrum. The rest of the project teams could develop functionality using a waterfall methodology. In that case, a simulation layer could be built by the Scrum teams from the initial waterfall architecture and design documentation. It would be enhanced as the waterfall design changed. However, no complete integration could be accomplished until the end of the waterfall, when overall integration testing could begin. The real software from the waterfall parts of the project then would replace the Scrum teams' simulation layer.

Summary

We've looked at some practices for integrating enterprise-wide Scrum engineering in this chapter. There are many other variations that might be required. Each variation should bring you closer to rapid development and release of functionality. You have to devise these solutions yourself, based on Scrum principles, best engineering practices, and common sense.

Start with an increment a month. Figure out what has to be done to make it shippable. Then reduce the length of the Sprint. Keep reducing the length. The solutions aren't as hard to figure out as they are to implement. You will know if the solution works by asking, "Have we moved our enterprise closer to being able to ship yesterday's work today?" If not, revise the solution and try again. You have a long row to hoe. Start now.

Chapter 8
People Practices

For the last 30 years, product management and development have been driven by predictive and functional practices. Because Scrum is radically different, the way people work with it is different. When you view the Scrum people practices recommended in this chapter, you might at first be taken aback. You might wonder how these practices could make sense. Your reaction isn't because current practices make sense or even work. They are just your current way of doing things. If you consider that they are the basis of your current problems with product management and development, changing them doesn't seem so unreasonable. When you consider the practices in this chapter, consider them on their own merit. Then, separately, consider the steps to adopt them.

Why are people willing to make the changes Scrum requires? We ask people to move out of a comfort zone into the unknown. They make the changes as a tradeoff to have work that is creative and enjoyable. It is an exchange for doing work in a way that makes sense. Moving out of your comfort zone is the cost for having customers who can't wait to get your products. It provides the reward of the joy of fulfilling work. To many, it is a fair trade.

This chapter addresses how Scrum teams do the enterprise's work, top to bottom. Chapters 6 and 7 described new ways to organize your work. Now we'll look at how you can form, care for, and feed the teams of people who will do the work.

#1: Organizing People to Do Enterprise Work

How do we organize our people to do our enterprise's work using Scrum?

Your enterprise's work can be organized, top to bottom, into a single Product Backlog. The organizing mechanism is a top-down decomposition of products, system architectures, or business operations. Figure 8-1 shows product decomposition by product, function, activity, and task.

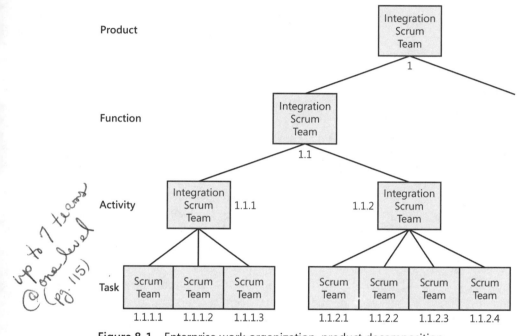

Figure 8-1   Enterprise work organization, product decomposition

People are organized in Scrum teams to mirror the organization of work. In Figure 8-1, a Scrum team exists at each node in the decomposition. Each Scrum team at each node is committed to its work. It is also responsible for directing and successfully integrating the work of its lower level nodes every Sprint. The work of any node is organized and prioritized at the next level up.

The bottom-most node is where most development occurs. Most Product Backlog requirements selected for Sprints relate to this level. *All other levels are integration or infrastructural development levels.* For instance, a component "Enter Telephone Number" is done at a node at the lowest level, such as 1.1.1.1. During a project, a Scrum team might be responsible for completing a Product Backlog item to change this component.

Product activities, such as "edit," consist of multiple modules. Activities, as outlined in Figure 8-2, are the next level of organization for the enterprise's work, people, and management.

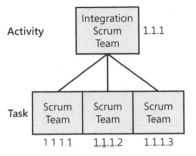

Figure 8-2   Activity-level organization

At the Activity level, an Integration Scrum team is responsible for managing all the work in its lower nodes. The lower levels are directed by the Activity-level Product Backlog, which is managed by the Activity-level Product Owner. For example, in Figure 8-2, the Integration Scrum team at node 1.1.1 is responsible for managing all the work of the Scrum teams at nodes 1.1.1.1, 1.1.1.2, and 1.1.1.3. The Integration Product Owner decomposes the Product Backlog for each of the Component-level Scrum teams. There is a Product Backlog for the node at 1.1.1. It is parsed to minimize dependencies and assigned to teams at the nodes of 1.1.1.1, 1.1.1.2, and 1.1.1.3.

The Integration-level Scrum development team doesn't develop functional software. It develops facilities to integrate, build, and test the work of the lower level Scrum teams. It builds infrastructural facilities to integrate these functions. The Integration-level development team also develops integration tests to confirm that all development at lower level nodes works. A general rule is that if any integration fails, the levels below must fix that integration prior to doing any new work. The Integration Scrum Team at 1.1.1 must demonstrate the integrated increments of the Scrum teams at 1.1.1.1, 1.1.1.2, and 1.1.1.3 at the Sprint Review. To do so, it must pull together the work of the Scrum teams at 1.1.1.1, 1.1.1.2, and 1.1.1.3 as frequently as possible, but no less than once per Sprint.

Integration-level teams can use the same ScrumMasters, Product Owners, and Scrum development team members. Sharing between the Component level and Integration level should be minimized to avoid task-switching overhead during actual development work. Sharing between Integration levels has fewer conflicts.

An organization of work at the Product level might look like Figure 8-3.

At the Product level, a Product Owner is responsible for maintaining an overall Product Backlog. For a specific release, he or she organizes a subset of the overall Product Backlog into a release Product Backlog. This Product Backlog is decomposed to pieces owned by lower node Product Owners. For instance, the Product Backlog owned by the Product Owner at the Integration Scrum Team of node 1 contains all the Product Backlog owned by the Product Owners at nodes 1.1 and 1.2. The Product Owner at node 1.1 contains all the Product Backlog owned by the Product Owners at nodes 1.1.1 and 1.1.2. This structure continues to the lowest level nodes. Product Owners, top to bottom, are responsible for the accuracy and timeliness of their part of the Product Backlog. To assist them, we usually have several people develop and groom the Product Backlog in some automated tool such as Microsoft Office Excel. These people can come from the old Project Management Office.

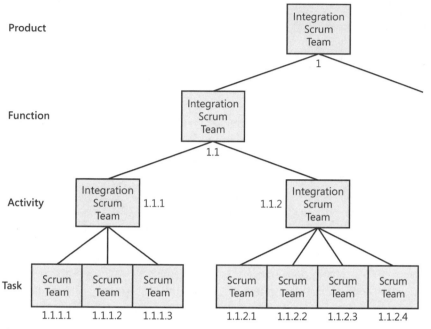

Figure 8-3   Product-level organization

The ScrumMaster on the Product-level team at node 1 is responsible for enforcing the rules and mechanisms of Scrum at that level and all lower levels. He or she ensures an integrated, tested build at the Product level for the Sprint Review at each level of nodes—Product, Function, Activity, and Task. The Product Owner plans, composes, distributes, and tracks work from his or her level down. The overall Product Backlog is owned and managed by the Product Owner on the Integration Scrum team at node 1. The higher the level is, the harder the Product Owner's and ScrumMaster's job is. The responsibility of Product-level jobs usually requires someone with Vice President–level or Director-level title and authority. Corresponding levels of responsibility and authority are required at higher and lower levels.

Daily Scrums are held at the lowest level nodes, such as 1.1.1.1. When multiple levels of Daily Scrums are conducted, this level is called S1. The higher level Daily Scrum of Scrums are called S2, S3, S4, and so forth and are held at each level. If there are more levels, they are numbered accordingly, but the bottom level node is always S1. Daily Scrums for levels above S1, also called *Daily Scrums of Scrums*, are meetings between representatives of all next-lower level teams to discuss the following four points:

- What did each team do yesterday?

- What will each team do tomorrow?

- What were other teams counting on our team finishing that remains undone?

- What is our team planning on doing that might affect other teams?

These Daily Scrum of Scrums meetings are working sessions that often last longer than 15 minutes. Their purpose is to uncover and remedy any dependency and integration issues between teams as rapidly as possible.

At the component level (S1) and activity level (S2), the Daily Scrums are indeed held daily. The attendees are people who are familiar with the engineering content of their area and can discuss tradeoffs with each other. At the Feature level, the S3 Scrums might be held every third day. At the Product level, the S4 Scrums are held weekly. At the Product Family level, the S5 Scrums are usually held no more often than monthly. If the higher levels are held too often, the amount of information passing from top to bottom and back, or *churn*, can overwhelm the entire process.

#2: Team Creation

How do I organize my people into Scrum teams?

The Product Owner and ScrumMaster are the first people on a Scrum team. They are responsible for selecting the Scrum development team members. To optimize the productivity of the team, the developers are selected based on three variables:

- People who have successfully worked together previously

- People who understand the product or business domain

- People who know how to use the selected technology

The team is also selected based on what constitutes a "done" increment. For instance, if user documentation is part of an increment, the team should have a technical writer.

These people can be selected from other, lower priority work teams. Or these people can be selected from something called the *bench*. The bench is where unassigned Scrum team members wait for work. They might be on the bench because their work has been completed or they were asked to leave their Scrum teams.

In a brand new Scrum adoption, we line up the Product Owners and ScrumMasters by the return on investment (ROI) and priority of their work and let them choose their teams from the bench. When no more people are left on the bench or nobody wants the remaining people, we stop forming teams. At the start of a release cycle or project, the Product Owners can form new teams based on the priority of their Product Backlog. They can stay with their existing teams, reformulate their teams, or get new teams. We, of course, first make them aware that productivity will significantly drop as a team reforms and renormalizes. Whenever possible, leave teams intact.

It is easy to think too much about who should be on a team. The best way to identify who should be on a team is for the team to make the decision itself. I ran into a situation that taught me this lesson.

Woodgrove Bank is a large financial institution whose primary service is banking. Woodgrove Bank had regional origins but had been growing through nationwide acquisitions of other banks. The teller systems in the acquired banks were different from Woodgrove Bank's teller system. All the teller systems were difficult to use. Woodgrove Bank formed a project to create a new teller system, Teller4U. A development group of 45 people was formed. The entire team reported to the vice president of development, Jack Creasey.

The Product Owner, Scott Culp, wanted frequent releases of Teller4U. Jack and Scott agreed that five releases in the first year would be appropriate, and that Scrum would be the best process to deliver them. Each release would be used by a prototype banking team to provide rapid feedback. In addition, the development group was using CVS, an easy-to-use, but limited source-code management system. CVS's weakness was that it didn't support simultaneous multirelease development very well.

Jack devised a way for the 45 developers to build the five releases within one year using CVS. Unfortunately, when I visited the teams, they hated the approach. They complained that it was inefficient, still only allowed two simultaneous copies of CVS, and wasn't working. When I discussed this with Jack, he asked me to devise a better process than his. He had wracked his brain, and it seemed pretty good to him. Then we remembered self-management. The people who do the work are supposed to figure out how to do it. We asked them to use Scrum. They were supposed to figure out how to do Teller4U from within the teams.

Jack and I met with all 45 developers. Jack reminded them that they were self-managing. This meant that they were to come up with the best team structure and internal processes for developing Teller4U using Scrum. The developers looked at us carefully. They were sure that they were being set up to take the blame. We ignored their looks. We then told the developers that we would be back in two hours to hear their approach for building the next release.

What if this didn't work? What if the developers weren't able to figure out how to do their work? What if 45 people were too many for self-management? What if we came back and they had done nothing for the two hours? Our expectations were low. We feared that no more than five or six of the lead developers would be in the conference room when we returned.

Much to our surprise, all 45 developers were in the conference room when we returned. The developers had also invited Scott and his manager of the prototype team into the meeting. The white boards were covered with schematics and the conference table littered with paper. The prototype team manager started by telling us that she wanted only two releases that year. She said that five releases were far too many to really work through, since they would be refining and testing various workflows as they tested each release. One of the lead developers then told us that they had figured out how to use Scrum to generate the two releases that year. In particular, one person from the prototype team would be on each Sprint team to help them make the best design decisions.

Jack asked how they were going to use CVS to do this. Speaking for all the developers, a lead developer told us that was none of our business. The team was self-managing and had figured out something that should work. If it stopped working because of an unexpected problem, they would be responsible for revising the approach so that they could deliver their commitments. We either trusted them to manage themselves or we didn't.

Jack and I left the conference room with Scott. We were treated to increments of Teller4U functionality every month, and two more releases that year. The project is now in its second year and doing fine.

#3: Team Work

The people in my enterprise aren't used to working in teams all the time. What can I do to prepare them?

Every Scrum team, regardless of its level in the enterprise, will go through the steps of forming, storming, norming, and performing.[1] This process is shown in Figure 8-4.

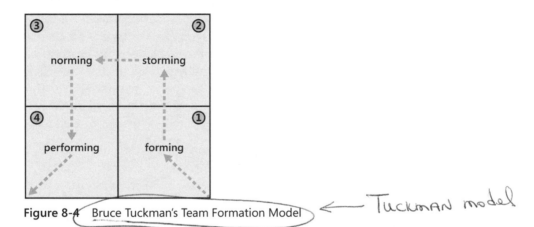

Figure 8-4   Bruce Tuckman's Team Formation Model   ← Tuckman model

When done formally and properly, the first step—formation—simplifies all subsequent steps. It arms the team for upcoming problems. The formation activity can be facilitated by the Human Resources Department or some other source of team-building expertise. During this activity, the team develops an identity, a way of working together, and a way to resolve conflicts. Use exercises based on real-life problems the team can expect to encounter. For example, I usually have a team work on how it will develop requirements and acceptance tests. The team members usually expect that the analyst will do the first requirements and the tester will do the testing. There are alternatives, but it is important for the team to figure out its first steps. At the end of the formation activity, the team should have a team name, it should have a definition of Sprint and Daily Scrum "done," as well as having formed rules of etiquette and engineering rules. The team should discuss and tentatively formalize their Sprint process for turning Product Backlog items into something "done."

---

1 Tuckman, Bruce W. (1965) "Developmental sequence in small groups," *Psychological Bulletin*, 63, 384–399.

The team also needs to be trained in how to resolve its inevitable conflicts. When the team starts Sprinting, it develops product. As it does so, professional conflicts about how to do so and personal conflicts about who does what will arise. This is the storming phase of the Tuckman model. The team will use its knowledge of conflict resolution to come up with agreements in the norming phase of the model. If the team is unable to do so, it draws again on the Human Resources Department or any other externally established source of help. These new agreements will be the basis of its ability to perform in the performing phase.

The performing phase is not permanent. Disagreements and conflict can be expected in the complexity of product development. The team will repeatedly fall back into the storming phase and need to come up with new norms of operation.

I remember walking toward a team room one day. The team had been working together for six weeks. As I approached the room, the lead analyst and lead engineer emerged from the room, yelling at each other and calling each other names. They then fled in separate directions before I could ask what was going on. I entered the team room and found the rest of the team shocked and withdrawn. The team's productivity was now zero. I asked what had happened. Apparently, before Scrum was adopted, the analysis group always wrote the functional specification and gave it to the engineers. The engineers then took liberty with the specification and wrote the system as they saw fit. The analysis group decried this, and the engineering group ignored them. This was a long-standing conflict in the enterprise. When we put people from the analysis and engineering group together on the team, they brought the problem and all the tension of it with them. The problem had now bubbled up and stopped the team dead in its tracks. Adequate training in conflict resolution or an external resource to help them could have resolved the conflict before it got out of hand.

#4: How People Are Managed

How do I manage people to meet enterprise objectives? Who is responsible for what? How do I ensure that things get done?

Scrum teams manage themselves, from the top to the bottom of the enterprise. You don't manage them to do things. You set goals. The teams manage themselves to build the Product Backlog and reach the goals. You inspect the results at the end of every Sprint and adapt accordingly.

To understand how to do this, let's consider a one-Scrum team company. The team reports to you, the CEO, to build and deploy product. The team consists of one Product Owner with one Product Backlog of work, one ScrumMaster, and a development team of eight developers. You manage the Product Owner and the ScrumMaster. The team is a single entity and manages itself. (All Scrum teams are self-managing.) However, it is answerable to the Product Owner for building the product. It is answerable to the ScrumMaster for following the Scrum process.

Your enterprise is successful. The product sells. Prospects clamor for more. Customers demand enhancements. You need to build more products quickly. You ask the existing Scrum team to add more people as rapidly as it can. It further decomposes and rearranges the Product Backlog so that subsets of it can be assigned to new teams. It figures four new Scrum teams can be immediately added.

All the Product Owners on the new teams will report to the initial Product Owner, who is responsible for optimizing overall return on investment and competitiveness. All the new ScrumMasters will report to the ScrumMaster on the original team, who will ensure that everyone knows how to use Scrum and does so. The new Scrum teams manage themselves. The initial Scrum development team is responsible for the work of all new Scrum teams. It has to be consistent and integrate into one high-quality product. The team devises an architecture within which more teams can work on individual pieces without stepping on each other. The team devises a set of coding and design standards to ensure consistency. The team also sets up a common development environment.

In Figure 8-5, each new Scrum team—such as 1.1, 1.2, and 1.3—has a nucleus of one person from the original Scrum team. He or she works with the new team's ScrumMaster and Product Owner to hire the rest of the developers. He or she is responsible for teaching the new people how systems are developed in your enterprise. New Scrum teams can be formed until at least one developer is left on the original Scrum team. The original team consists of these remaining developers and the original Product Owner and ScrumMaster. This team now becomes an Integration Scrum team, responsible for the work of all subordinate nodes.

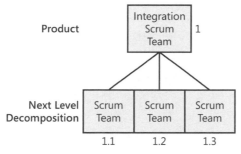

Figure 8-5   Example of an Activity-level organization

The enterprise continues to succeed. More and more people are hired. They are interviewed and hired by the Product Owner, ScrumMasters, and Scrum development team, such as at 1.1. The Scrum team at 1.1 forms lower level Scrum teams, such as 1.1.1 and 1.1.2. Each new team consists of a Product Owner, ScrumMaster, and development team. The new Scrum development teams are seeded with people from the parent node, such as 1.1. As the enterprise fleshes out, it looks like Figure 8-6.

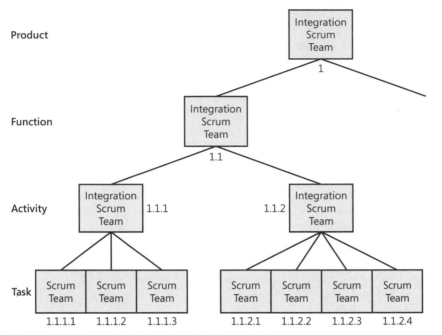

Figure 8-6   Example of a Product-level organization

The Product Owner at the very top of the hierarchy, node 1, is responsible for overall Product ROI and success. The ScrumMaster at node 1 is responsible for Scrum being used effectively throughout the enterprise. This ScrumMaster is also responsible for overall enterprise change. At each node in the hierarchy, the Scrum development teams report to the Product Owner to find out what work to do, and to the ScrumMaster for instructions on following the Scrum process and facilitating change.

The ScrumMaster is responsible for teaching the Product Owner how to most effectively manage the work of the Scrum team using the Product Backlog, Sprint Planning Meeting, and the Sprint Review Meeting. He or she teaches the Product Owner how to maximize ROI and meet their objectives through Scrum. The ScrumMaster is also responsible for improving the lives of the development team by facilitating creativity and empowerment. He or she is responsible for improving the productivity of the development team in any way possible. Also, the ScrumMaster is responsible for working with teams to improve the engineering practices and tools so that each increment of functionality is potentially shippable. When people aren't fulfilling their roles, the person held accountable is the ScrumMaster. He or she hasn't taught the team how to do their work.

The development teams are responsible for managing themselves. Every Sprint, they evaluate their processes for opportunities to improve them. They are required to follow all the conventions, architectures, and standards devised by the original Scrum team. As these evolve, the development teams are responsible for staying conversant with them and continuing to follow them. They are also responsible for integrating their work with all higher levels at least once a Sprint.

*the bench

Sometimes the new hires don't work out. When they degrade team performance or productivity, the team is responsible for removing them. The team tells them that they are no longer needed. The "purged" person goes to the bench. They can be selected from the bench by another team looking for new members. If they are on the bench too long, Human Resources is responsible for placing them elsewhere in the enterprise. Teams are very reluctant to remove anyone, however. They are a social group that tends to be very forgiving and caring.

Offsetting team reluctance to remove team member is the Product Owner's need for productivity. If the Product Owner's development team isn't productive enough, the anticipated return on investment can't be achieved. He or she then meets with the ScrumMaster to replace or reformulate the existing team. On one project I was involved with, the ScrumMaster removed four members of a seven-person team and productivity soared. When this isn't possible, the Product Owner might have to cancel the project.

Sometimes people on the development team or the Product Owner won't or can't comply with Scrum. The ScrumMaster must replace them. They must be removed before they drag down the entire team, process, and enterprise. The tactics for removing a Product Owner are often sticky. However, the absence of a Product Backlog or Product Backlog burn-down is a compelling reason to do so. Worse, creation of irrelevant or off-target increments, Sprint by Sprint, with no correction is appalling. The ScrumMaster is responsible for teaching the Product Owner how to do his or her job. If the raw material is weak, the ScrumMaster can't let failure to comply with Scrum persist for more than two Sprints.

Sometimes ScrumMasters are ineffective. They don't teach the Product Owner how to manage the Product Backlog. They don't teach the team how to self-manage. They continue to use command-and-control techniques. They should be removed by the ScrumMaster they report to. Sometimes Scrum development teams are ineffective. They can't build enough product to meet the Product Owner's needed return on investment. The Product Owner should either work with the ScrumMaster to reformulate the team or cancel the project. Sometimes the Product Owners don't meet the return on investment required by the Product Owner they report to. That Product Owner should replace them.

A Scrum reporting structure for an enterprise is shown in Figure 8-7.

The Product Owners report to each other, up through the hierarchy of nodes. At each node, the Scrum development team reports to the Product Owner regarding what work to do and the ScrumMaster for instruction on conforming with the Scrum process. This reporting relationship is unusual because the team manages itself. The Product Owner is only responsible for telling the Scrum development team what to do at the start of every Sprint in the Sprint Planning Meeting. The Product Owner doesn't manage or review the individual team members. He or she inspects the team's work only at the Sprint Review. The Scrum development team similarly reports to the ScrumMaster for compliance with the Scrum process. ScrumMasters report to the ScrumMaster at the next higher node, up through the hierarchy of nodes.

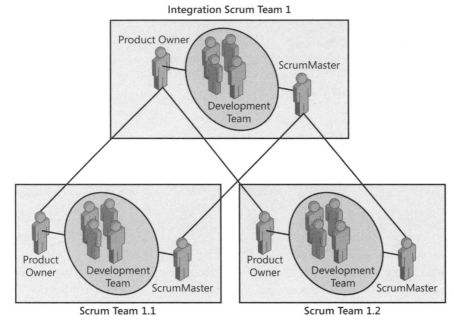

Figure 8-7 Scrum reporting relationships

#5: Functional Expertise

My development organization has different functional skills, such as systems architecture, usability engineering, programming quality assurance, and technical writing. People with these skills used to be managed by a functional manager. Now these functional managers are ScrumMasters, Product Owners, or Scrum development team members. How do I ensure that the functional skills are kept at the highest levels?

I recommend that you set aside a part of every employee's time to pursue activities that are outside their current Scrum teams and that benefit the enterprise. I recommend an allowance of 20 percent of their time. Let the people coalesce into interest groups where they work together. Some of this time can be spent working with peers in sustaining and enhancing functional expertise. Some of the work can be researching and prototyping new ideas. The yellow sticky notes of 3M and Gmail at Google were developed in this way. Twenty percent of everyone's time might seem like a big investment for your enterprise. If you add up all the time you used to invest in functional organizations, it will be modest by comparison. Try this approach and be prepared to be surprised, as Google and 3M were.

People form functional expertise groups around systems architecture, quality, programming, refactoring, and any other development expertise. They will define standards, guidelines, and conventions for such enterprise work. These groups will also define career paths within that discipline within the enterprise, and criteria and tests for advancing along the career path. They also might want to be available as a recruiter and interviewer of new people. These groups emerge based on mutual interest. These groups self-manage functional expertise within the enterprise. They do not have a manager.

All of these groups use Scrum. They elect Product Owners, ScrumMasters, and teams. They spell their work out in a Product Backlog.

#6: Compensation

How do I compensate and reward people for their work? Does the team structure change anything?

Two variables control a person's pay. Base salary of an employee is directly proportional to his or her responsibility and accountability. Directors earn a higher base pay than supervisors. Lead programmers earn a higher base pay than junior programmers. The greater the salary, the more that is expected of them.

The second variable is the performance of enterprise, the big team. You can reward all teams' performances from a common pot of funds. The source of the funds is all money that would otherwise have been allocated to bonuses or individual incentive pay. Use this pot of funds to reward team performance toward enterprise goals. The incentive pay is distributed through a team to its members proportionally according to base salary. If one team member makes $x and another makes $2x, the team bonus is split so that the person making $2x gets twice as much of it as the person making $x. This allocation is based on the assumption that someone with a base pay that is twice as much as another person has knowledge and skills twice as valuable. The person who allocates the team bonus is the Product Owner. This starts at the top of the enterprise and is allocated downward according to performance.

#7: Extra Managers

I've assigned people to be ScrumMasters, Product Owners, and part of Scrum development teams. There are still some extra managers. What do they do?

Almost all the product management and development work is done in a hierarchy of Scrum teams. Unless remaining staff and managers have other solid work to do, their idle hands are the devil's workshop. They interfere with the Scrum teams.

I visited several Wingtip, Inc. teams at their Sprint Planning Meetings. Strangely, their managers were in attendance. The team members sat in silence, while the managers investigated the work, asked questions of the team members, committed the team to the Sprint goal, and then broke down and assigned the work. No self-management occurred. The productivity and joy of teamwork was forgone.

I investigated and found that 18 first- and second-level managers were still unassigned. They didn't want to be ScrumMasters. They still wanted the prestige and authority of their old jobs. I gathered them together. I asked them what their responsibilities were regarding the people who reported to them and who were also in Scrum teams. The things they told me they were responsible for included ensuring there was no slack time, that the work was appropriate, and that the people were doing their work correctly.

Of course, these weren't self-managing teams. Scrum development team members still reported outside their Scrum team. Worse, until their managers found other meaningful work, they would continue to manage the people who still reported to them.

#8: Teams with Distributed Members

The people in some of my teams aren't collocated. What do I do?

If people on a team haven't worked together, they don't trust each other. They don't know what the other person is likely to do. They can't anticipate how to work with them.

One company had a team that had members in Lithuania, Finland, the UK, Pennsylvania, and Alabama. The entire team gathered at headquarters in Pennsylvania with the Product Owner to plan the release. They stayed together for the first one or two Sprints of the release to iron out the highest value and architectural issues. Then the team members went back to their offices. They continued to use the same shared development environment. They had their offices connected all the time by Internet-enabled intercom. Whenever anyone had a question, he or she would just lean over to the intercom and ask it of whomever was nearby. If nobody was present, the employee would use instant messaging or e-mail.

Daily Scrums were still 15 minutes long. Everyone would call in on a conference call. The call often extended past the Daily Scrum as design and testing issues were worked out. For each Sprint Review and Planning meeting, at least half the team would gather again in Pennsylvania with the Product Owner.

Another company had a team that was evenly split between New York City and China. They followed the same team practices as the team just mentioned, but the time-zone differences made the Daily Scrums hard to schedule. The team decided to form representative teams. One person in China represented the rest of the Chinese at the Daily Scrum for the first week. For the next week, one person in New York represented the rest of the New Yorkers at the Daily Scrum. The person representing his or her location was then responsible for communicating with the rest of the team at their location.

I not only have teams with distributed members, but my teams are distributed in different locations. What do I do?

These teams are required to integrate their work into one demonstrable increment at least once every Sprint Review Meeting. To do so, they probably will have to integrate and test their work at least weekly, and perhaps daily. Integration will require them to work together through several Sprints to resolve differences and use the same design. The teams will devise the best mechanisms to do so if and only if they are held accountable for one integrated increment. The mechanics of integration across teams are thoroughly discussed in Chapter 7, "Engineering Practices."

#9: Scarce Skills Needed by Many Teams

Only a few people have certain skills. They are needed by many teams at once. I know everyone on a team should be full time, but how do I handle this?

Three Scrum teams had work that originated from the same Product Backlog. The teams used the same development environment. Every team needed the same database administrator (DBA) full time for the next several Sprints. They asked me to tell them what to do. I investigated the Product Backlog with the Product Owner. Each team's work was about the same priority as the other teams. Remembering the wisdom of Solomon, I told the teams to split the DBA's time, 33 percent to each team.

At the next Sprint Planning Meeting, the teams told me that my solution didn't work. The teams all needed the DBA the same time during their Sprints. I was embarrassed. My solution hadn't worked. I wracked my mind for a better solution. Then I remembered that these teams were supposed to manage themselves. I asked them to spend the next hour and devise their own solution. At the end of the hour, the teams had agreed that the DBA would spend most of her time with the team where her work was most critical. However, she would mentor and coach several people on the other teams for all their DBA work. Most critically, they said that no team would commit to any work unless the DBA was in that team's Sprint Planning Meeting and also committed. As a result, all three teams had their Sprint Planning Meeting in the same room at the same time.

The team's solution became a general practice for Scrum teams with external dependencies. The external dependency can be a scare resource, another team, or an external vendor. Regardless, a team cannot commit to Sprint work unless the external dependency is in the Sprint Planning Meeting and also commits.

People who represent scarce resources often argue that they need to do their work in isolation, separate from the teams that will use their work. They argue that they are more effective than if they were on Scrum teams. Whenever this is done, the scarcity becomes amplified.

Their separation from the people who use their work increases and miscommunications grow. Mentoring and cross-training disappear. The best solution is to have them be part of the teams that use their work. They then might see new solutions that are better than those derived in isolation. As they work within the team, the team members learn from them.

Sometimes there just aren't enough resources for the work that is desired. The teams can't devise clever solutions that fully mitigate the shortage. Then you have a real constraint that must be addressed by slowing down the teams to cross-train them. You can hire additional people, but they too have a learning curve before the constraint is lessened and removed.

The Relationship Between Product Management/Customer and the Development Team

Until recently, I viewed this relationship as one of many changes in a Scrum adoption. I now view it as the most critical change, the lynchpin of the adoption. If this change is successful, the use of Scrum will persist and benefits will increase. If this change isn't successful, the use of Scrum in your enterprise might well unravel.

Many enterprises can't develop and release products as quickly as they would like. The lengthened release cycle impairs them competitively. Surprisingly, the cause can be traced to the relationship between an enterprise's product managers/customers and their developers. This relationship is deeply ingrained. Product Owners cherish their half of the relationship. It is the only way they know to get releases done on time. Developers just do whatever is needed to keep the Product Owners happy. This relationship changes when you adopt Scrum. The Product Owner is asked to manage a project to optimize value. The developers are asked to be open and honest about their progress even if it disappoints the Product Owner.

In this chapter, I'll present a way you can shorten the time to release through managing value. The results will not only be faster development, but higher quality and less expensive development. I'll then present the impact and consequences of your current customer and developer relationship on your enterprise. We'll look at something called the infrastructure and its role in your woes. We'll then explore some accelerators that might shorten your development cycle in conjunction with Scrum. Finally, I'll expose the origins of the problem in the traditional customer and developer relationship so that you can guard against its recurrence.

#1: Shortening the Time to Release Through Managing Value

We have to commit to delivery dates. The enterprise has promised the next release to key customers, and we have to deliver on time to keep them. How do we do that using Scrum?

Scrum introduces the possibility of value-driven development. We usually control projects through four variables:

1. The functionality we want and the work needed to build it

2. The time for delivering the functionality, or the due date

3. The cost of the project

4. The quality of the functionality

Scrum introduces a fifth variable, value. We can shorten delivery dates and reduce costs by optimizing the value of the project. We optimize value by delivering the highest value increments of functionality first. We stop delivering increments when the value is less than the cost. We also stop delivering increments when the opportunity value is greater than the marginal value of the next increment.

A project used to be "done" when all the functionality that we could think of was delivered. Statistics show that at least 65 percent of this expensive, hard-won functionality is rarely or never used.[1] Think of the most common desktop software. Most of the lower menu paths are rarely or never navigated. Regardless, the vendors paid to build them and continue to pay to maintain them. For example, suppose the Product Owner estimates the cost to deliver the release at $1,000,000. It can be done in 10 months. The entire project has a return on investment (ROI) of 28 percent. Some of the functionality makes a significant contribution to the ROI, and other pieces don't. If the Product Owner knew which functionality were ROI drags, he or she would not build them. The Product Owner might be able to deliver an improved ROI by spending only $350,000 and delivering in four months. This is an example of judiciously managing to optimize value. This is value-driven release management.

Optimizing value is straightforward with Scrum. The first step is to establish a baseline plan representing the functionality to be delivered. It is organized as an estimated, prioritized Product Backlog. Capacity, or *development velocity*, is then estimated. Divide the total work of the Product Backlog by the monthly capacity. The result is the estimated number of months for the entire project and the estimated completion date. Personnel costs are calculated from total utilized capacity. The project starts toward these goals, and the Product Owner monitors its progress, Sprint by Sprint. A full description of this approach is in my earlier book, *Agile Project Management with Scrum* (Microsoft Press, 2004).

---

1 Jim Johnson, *My Life Is Failure* (The Standish Group International, Inc., 2006)

Sometimes project progress doesn't meet the baseline plan. The estimates were wrong. The team's velocity was lower then expected. Changes were needed. The baseline date is in danger. The Product Owner can monitor this, as shown in Figure 9-1, by tracking the burn-down of remaining Product Backlog work.

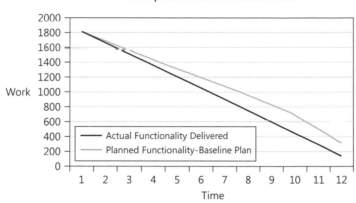

Figure 9-1   Deviation from the baseline plan

At the end of the third Sprint, less work has been completed than expected. The Product Owner has early warnings of schedule variance. He or she can adjust everyone's expectations accordingly. This is similar to an enterprise's financial and sales plans when a forecast becomes a baseline plan. Everyone synchronizes their work to the forecast. On a monthly basis, actual results are compared to forecast and the enterprise adjusts. The actual results might not be what are desired, but we can take early action. Now we can do the same adjustment with development projects.

The Product Owner manages value to control a project's end date. By re-evaluating and restructuring the content of the project, the overall work can be reduced. He or she prioritizes the functionality as the Product Backlog changes so that the most valuable work is always the highest priority. As each increment is done, the Product Owner evaluates it. When the anticipated value starts reducing ROI, the project can be stopped. The functionality can then be shipped and the enterprise can start benefiting sooner than expected.

Relative Valuation with Scrum

It is hard to determine the ROI of individual pieces of functionality. For instance, how much more revenue will accrue if we spend $270,000 to develop functionality to import a prior year's tax data? To compensate for this difficulty, we can use the statistical technique of relative valuation. We can provide the Product Owner with 1,000 imaginary Ping-Pong balls. Larger projects get more. We ask him or her to allocate them among the Product Backlog based on the importance of each item toward meeting goals of the release. Some items are really, really important and get most of the Ping-Pong balls. Surprisingly, most of the Ping-Pong balls go to only 35 percent of the functionality. The hypothetical Product Backlog demonstrates this in Figure 9-1a.

PRODUCT BACKLOG	VALUE	EFFORT
Item 1	80	13
Item 2	75	34
Item 3	75	21
Item 4	74	13
. . .	. . .	. . .
Item 28	10	34
Item 29	8	13

Figure 9-1a   Product Backlog Value Distribution

Relative valuation of Product BacklogScrum teams turn the Product Backlog into shippable increments of functionality. We can track the relative value of the functionality delivered in each increment, counted in Ping-Pong balls. We can track the accumulated value delivered across time in a graph, as shown in Figure 9-2.

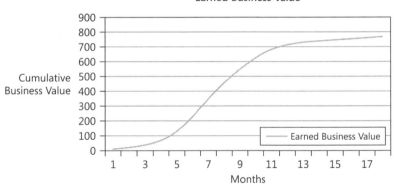

Figure 9-2   Cumulative value curve

At the start, cumulative value rises slowly as infrastructure and the development environment are put in place. The cumulative value then rises quickly as the highest value Product Backlog item is completed. When lower priority Product Backlog items are delivered, the accumulation of value slows.

This technique works if the number of Ping-Pong balls, or relative value, remains constant throughout the project. However, the total amount of value can increase or decrease as the Product Backlog changes. The cumulative value delivered for each Sprint must then be recalculated to a new baseline.

> **Tip**   Here is a formula you can use to help re-baseline the relative value of all Product Backlog items whenever the total value changes:
>
> ```
> ((new total value/last total value) * old accumulated value at that Sprint =
> new cumulative value at that Sprint)
> ```

For example, if the baseline value is 1,000 and we add a Product Backlog item with a value of 200, the total new value is 1,200. If we had delivered 200, 380, and 500 points of value in the first three Sprints, these would be reevaluated to the following:

```
(1200/1000)*200, (1200/1000)*380, and (1200/1000)*500
```

The Product Owner can now track both project progress and cumulative value delivered to optimize the project's value. For instance, in Figure 9-3, the enterprise wants to start using the product at the end of month 20. A trend line drawn at month 10 indicates a later completion date to be likely. The cumulative earned value curve in Figure 9-2, though, shows the cumulative value slope dropping by month 10. When the slope is less than 1, it could indicate there is an opportunity for value-driven development. The Product Owner could stop the project. In this example, lower value functionality is removed from the project and the remaining amount of work drops. At the average velocity, the project can now be completed by month 20. By directing work to maximize ROI, the Product Owner has met the enterprise's objectives. He or she has used Scrum to optimize value.

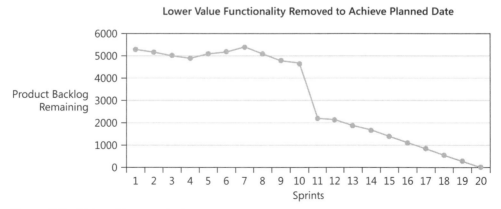

Figure 9-3   Value-driven project

#2: Just Do It

We tried value-driven management. We've massaged the requirements to eliminate low-value Product Backlog requirements. We're still not going to hit the date. There is too much to do. In the past, we've asked development to work harder. We tell them to do what it takes. They've always come through for me. Is this OK in Scrum?

What a dilemma! We have a budget. We need to get the release to the customers on that date, and we can't remove any more requirements without violating their expectations. Why can't we do what we've always done—just tell the developers to do it?

Developers can increase the amount of functionality they build if they reduce the quality of the functionality. Reducing quality is a time-honored tradition. Why not? As one product manager pointed out to me, "Quality is intangible!" This tradition operates as follows. We ask for more functionality or changes. The developers tell us it will take more time. We say that is too much time. The developers protest. We escalate to their management. We tell management, "The developers aren't on board, they aren't part of the team, and they are slacking off." The manager of the developers then tells them to "do it." And, by golly, it works! They do it.

The developers reduce quality by eliminating careful construction of design and logic. They don't review code for flaws. They don't create or run adequate tests. They work 12 to 14 hours a day and on weekends. They hack out something that kind of works. Developers can increase the amount of functionality delivered by a factor of three, in the short term. Cutting quality usually works for a single project. However, it should be used only in extreme circumstances. Afterward, the quality needs to be restored immediately. The cost you can use is $4 to remediate every $1 of dropped quality. Dropping quality might seem like a good short-term fix, but it decreases the value of an enterprise asset. Its repeated use has significant negative effects on the enterprise.

#3: The Infrastructure, or Core

Even cutting quality didn't do it. We can build new functionality satisfactorily; however, it takes us much longer to build functionality in our core products, or infrastructure. How do we arrange this work using Scrum to meet our deadlines?

Almost every enterprise that I've worked with shares a common engineering problem. It revolves around the enterprise's "core" or "infrastructure" or "legacy" product. The core is the heart of all the software or products for that enterprise. It is the common, basic functionality of all its products. It is where the common shared databases, transaction processing, and functionality reside. These enterprises can rapidly build new functionality. However, much of the new functionality also requires changes in the core. The problem is that the core takes a long time to change or modify. For every one hour spent building new functionality, ten hours have to be spent enhancing core functionality. Hundreds of developers might be held up waiting for core functionality changes.

The impact of core functionality on development projects is expressed in the following exercise. We need to release a new feature to our customers within three months. Three pieces of functionality are needed and consist of the following work:

- Function 1: 20 units of work—15 of new code and 5 in the core
- Function 2: 40 units of work—25 in the new code and 15 in the core
- Function 3: 30 units of work—20 in the new code and 10 in the core

We have made measurements and know that our ability to build functionality has the following characteristics:

- New functionality can be built at a velocity of 15 units of work per Sprint per team. As many teams as desired can be put on this work because no pre-existing knowledge is needed.

- Core functionality can be built at a velocity of 5 units of work per Sprint, total. This is the maximum velocity. It can't be increased. There is nobody else within the enterprise who can successfully work on the core.

How do we arrange the teams to meet the three-month release date? Upon inspection, it appears possible. We usually just increase the number of people working on a project to make a date possible. However, the core velocity constrains this approach. There is no way we can make this happen. We can get either function 1 and 3, or function 2, completed in three months, but no more. We are stuck.

This problem intrigued me. Why was the core development velocity so low? Why was the core so hard to modify? I found that all cores had the following common characteristics:

- They were fragile because they were poorly engineered. They have duplicated code, overly complex code, code plastered on top of other code, undocumented code, and code that didn't follow any standards. Documentation is nil or almost useless. Whenever a change is made to the core, something is likely to break elsewhere in the core.

- Inadequate tests were available to check that the core product still worked after modification. When tests were available, they were rarely automated. Retesting took a very, very long time.

- Only a handful of developers were left that were still competent to make modifications to the core. Even fewer were willing to do so. Everyone else had retired, died, or gone on to more interesting work.

I refer to core products with these characteristics as being "dead." It is very hard to get life from them. How did the core get this way? The process is well known to all of us. It is inherent in the traditional customer and development relationship. That the process builds dead cores is less well known. Let's look at how this happens.

We visited Wingtip in Chapter 7, in the "#1: Multilayer System Work Organized by Functionality" section. Wingtip's situation had become worse since the time of that anecdote, with further deterioration to its core. Several more core developers had left. However, the competitive pressure on the advertisement serving product had grown more severe. Ten Scrum development teams were assigned to add new functionality in a product road map. The road map called for 160 new or enhanced pieces of functionality. The teams estimated that 33 percent of all work would have to be done in the core.

I was attending a Sprint Review when I noticed something funny. The teams were demonstrating functionality without required changes to the core. They had segregated the approximately 33-percent core functionality changes into another Product Backlog. This work would be done later. As a consequence, what was demonstrated couldn't be adopted and wasn't done.

Only one team was able to demonstrate fully working functionality. It had developed an application programming interface (API) around the core. New functionality called on the core through the API. Rather than modify the core, the team rebuilt parts of the core into the API. The team even put a new database management system in the API. The core effectively now existed in two places. This created a conundrum for any further development. Did just the core have to be updated? Or did the API have to be updated also? You can imagine the chaos if all 10 teams had followed this approach.

We restructured the Sprint Planning Meeting to make the velocity constraint of the core more visible. We brought all the Product Owners, ScrumMasters, and developers for the 10 teams into a large room. We asked the Product Owners to collectively prioritize all their work. Then, in priority order, each Product Owner and lead engineer got to form a team for the next Sprint, including the necessary core developers. As each team was formed, we asked the people on it to leave the room. Ten pieces of functionality were selected. Then there were no more core developers left. No more new teams could be formed. Forty people remained. If they built new functionality, it would be unusable. We had them start building test harnesses for the core, hoping to make it more stable.

#4: Accelerators to Recovery

Scrum seems to have improved the productivity in most parts of development. But it hasn't improved infrastructure development productivity. Since almost all of our work involves changing the infrastructure, how do we improve productivity there? We may not be able to deliver products any faster if we can't solve this problem.

Many enterprises already have a dying core. You can figure out how bad the impact of the core on the enterprise is by modeling the following items:

- The cost and time needed to rebuild the core. (See the alternative approaches presented next.) The cost and time depend on the skills and availability of existing core developers and on the degradation of the core. They also depend on how good the rebuilt core has to be and what velocity it has to support.

- The rapidity with which the enterprise is losing market share.

- The tolerance of the enterprise's customer base to the increasingly poor quality of its products.

The following list details several alternatives to restore life to the core:

- **Remediate the core.**   Restore the quality to the core product. Form new teams to redesign and refactor the code. Write overall design information to guide navigation in the code. Develop automated test harnesses that ensure the core is working. This approach can be compared to rebuilding a house that has fallen into severe disrepair. It usually is quicker, cheaper, and safer to tear it down. Unfortunately, as core functions are remediated, you will have to make assumptions about how the new code should work. Many functions use the core and there rarely is a complete inventory. Because all the usages are unknown, it might be impossible to devise complete functional tests.

- **Strangle the core.**   As the engineers enhance or fix bugs in the core, allocate enough time for them to rewrite that area with a good design and clean, commented code. Bit by bit, the new code will strangle the design dead code.

- **Rewrite the core.**   Understand what functions the core performs. Rewrite them from scratch. This approach suffers many of the problems of remediation. You might never know what has been done wrong or not done at all until the customers tell you. You will also have to synchronize any interim changes between the new and old core.

- **Prop up the core.**   Live with the core longer but with less damage. Understand as much functionality of the core as possible. You should document as much design and mapping as possible. Build automated test harnesses around the core so that you will know when it breaks. As any piece of core functionality needs enhancing, rewrite it from scratch. This approach is better than the first two, but it is still highly risky.

- **Drain the pond.**   Rebuild the core in new technology with good design and test harnesses. Rewrite pieces of core functionality one at a time in the new technology. Move known users of the core functionality to the new core one by one. Assure that each user of the core functionality works and that tests are in the core test harness. When all known users of a piece of core functionality are converted, try turning off that part of the core. Find the other users, one by one, as they complain.

#5: The Mother of All Problems

How did our enterprise get in this pickle of a dying core? We have excellent developers. We have a great marketing department. We have good market share and are loved by our customers. We are respected in the industry. Where did this come from, and how did it happen?

The methods of improving the core are expensive, risky, and time-consuming. You might be shocked. Earlier, in the section "#1: Shortening the Time to Release Through Managing

Value," we looked at how you can avoid the problem. But how and why did it occur originally? We have to look at our traditions and habits to fully understand this so that we don't repeat ourselves.

Most enterprises initiate a project by estimating the cost and delivery date. Customers provide input by defining everything that they want done—the requirements. Each step thereafter decomposes customer requirements into the ultimate product. Changes become more expensive as the decomposition progresses. If 60 percent of the project is complete, many of its internal workings are complete. They are interrelated and depend on each other. A change at the start of a project might cost one dollar. When the product is in production and has already been shipped, the same change costs 100 dollars.[2]

An average of 35 percent of the requirements change during a project. Many of these changes occur late in the project. This puts the customer in a bind. Development tells them that changes jeopardize the initial estimated dates and costs. The customers want the changes, but not if they cause cost overruns or delivery date slippages.

Accurately predicting a date and total cost at the start of a project is very difficult. The sheer complexity of the requirements and the changes are unpredictable. The vagaries of the technologies employed often aren't yet known. The people doing the work cause huge variances between predictions and actual results. This is a dilemma for customers who have acquired enough funding to support an expected cost and date. They expect to get benefits on that date. Customers become increasingly frustrated as developers resist changes. Project costs and delivery dates keep changing, always upwards. Developers are embarrassed to tell customers that things have slipped again because they couldn't fit an ever-increasing amount of work into the same size date/cost box.

A dysfunctional relationship between customers and developers arises. Customers rely on telling the developers to "just do it," while tolerating modest slippage of cost and date. The developers then have to do more work in less time. They cut quality so that they can do more work. The resulting functionality might wind up in the core, making the core harder to enhance and maintain. Fewer enhancements can be planned. Longer development cycles are needed. The enterprise becomes less competitive.

I can tell whether an enterprise is heading toward a dead core. Decreasing development velocity is the first sign. Teams are able to do less work in the same time because of lowered quality. A reduced velocity curve is shown in Figure 9-4.

---

2 Barry W. Boehm, *Software Engineering Economics* (Prentice Hall, 1981)

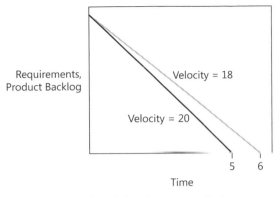

Figure 9-4   Reduced development velocity

You can track a core dying. You can see in Figure 9-4 that in the fifth release of a product, the velocity was 18 functional requirements (per $100,000 expended). The customers and developers developed a baseline plan. The plan portrayed an estimated completion date. The customers wanted the release sooner and pressured the developers to do whatever it takes. The developers accommodated them by dropping the quality. With lowered quality, the team was able maintain a short-term velocity of 20 functional requirements per $100,000. They met the date.

During the sixth release, the development velocity was only 16. The reduced quality from the fifth release produced product that was harder to change and more fragile. Work went more slowly. The customers again became upset and pressured the developers to not let this slip. The developers dropped quality again and achieved a short-term velocity of 18.

During the seventh release, the baseline velocity was 14. The developers were having a hard time making changes and keeping the core running. Customers felt that the developers must really be slacking off. The customers pressured them again. This wasn't pleasant, but what could they do? Also, this had worked the last two times. So the developers dropped quality again and achieved a short-term velocity of 16.

The core was getting more and more difficult to modify. It was poorly designed. It had code slapped on. It didn't have any organized structure. It didn't follow standards. You can project the pattern shown in Figure 9-5. Short-term productivity in a project is increased by dropping quality. As a result, the core quality drops. The next project takes longer to do the same work. Under time and cost pressures, quality is dropped again. Each subsequent release has a lower velocity. The customers are more frustrated because of the lowered velocity. The pressure to do more is repeated. The result is a vicious cycle that progressively degrades the quality of the core. The customers become more frustrated. The developers become more dissatisfied.

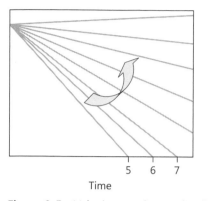

Time

Figure 9-5 Velocity trend curve leading to a dead core

You can see how we have built our own dead core–fragile, untested, and with fewer developers working on it–release by release. Less functionality can be developed for the same cost in each progressive release. Enterprises can create dead cores within five years.

Another factor progressively slows velocity. As the product becomes more fragile, more bugs and defects are found after it is shipped. The developers have to fix these defects while building the next release. Increasing effort and cost are spent maintaining each release. This is a double whammy: the developers have a more difficult product to enhance, and they also have less time to do the enhancements. Customer anxiety further increases. Customers increase the pressure for developers to do more and speed down the slippery slope.

Figure 9-6 depicts the maintenance curve for a dead core. Maintenance is reasonable at first, but with each progressive poor quality release, it increases. A maintenance curve such as that shown in Figure 9-7 presages a dead core. We can suspect that the enterprise also has the decreased velocity curve of Figure 9-5. We can be sure that the enterprise embodies a dysfunctional relationship between customers and developers.

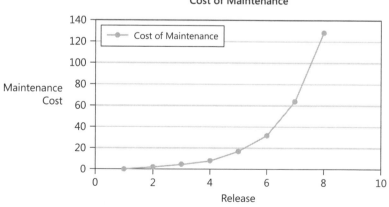

Figure 9-6 Maintenance cost curve

What are the competitive consequences to the enterprise? I graphed the velocity of enhancing core functionality at several enterprises. I then graphed the velocity of building new functionality. The graph looked like Figure 9-7.

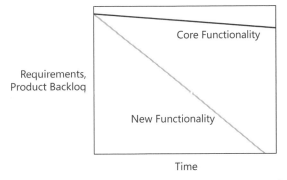

Figure 9-7   Velocity of core functionality and new functionality

In Figure 9-7, the velocity for new functionality averages 20 pieces of functionality per $100,000. The velocity for core functionality averages 1 piece of functionality per $100,000. All new development could be constrained to the velocity of core development. To remove the constraint, we usually can increase the number of core developers. Unfortunately, very few people in an enterprise know how to work on the core. There aren't any more people that we can add to the core team. Once, when this wasn't recognized, the core team was increased from eight to over 100. The core velocity dropped rather than increased because the original eight infrastructure developers had to cope with the other 100 people.

A dead core is not good for an enterprise. Competition can quickly introduce new, compelling functionality and the enterprise with the dead core can't respond. As we watch enterprises today, we can easily name Company A and B. Company A's primary product is an Internet portal. This company is driving all of its competitors mad. It frequently introduces sophisticated new functionality. None of its competitors can match its speed of introduction. I have worked at Company A and at its competitors. Company A isn't better. Its engineers are no smarter. However, Company A is relatively new and its code base is still clean. Its competitors have been in business longer. Their code bases are close to dead. Unfortunately, Company A is arrogant. It believes it competes better because it is better. Based on my work at Company A, I give it another four years before its core is almost dead.

This is also true in the insurance industry. One insurance company, Company B, is rapidly taking market share from old-line companies. It rapidly introduces new insurance products. The other companies can't respond. Company B has a new code base. It also religiously uses Agile techniques to retain the quality of the code base.

The health of an enterprise rides on resolving this problem. The root of the change is the relationship between product management and the development organization.

Part III
Appendices

Appendix A
Scrum 1, 2, 3

This appendix summarizes Scrum. Scrum is devised specifically to wrest usable products from complex problems. It has been used successfully on thousands of projects in hundreds of organizations over the last 16 years. It is based in industrial process control theory, whose mechanisms have been used to create complex products successfully since time began. Industrial process control theory employs empirical processes that depend on such little-understood mechanisms as self-organization and emergence.

The Science

Product development is a complex endeavor. This isn't unusual because the universe is full of complexity. Most complexities we don't know about; others we are content to leave alone. Some, like pressure turning coal into diamonds, take care of themselves. And others we can use with a level of imprecision such that the complexity doesn't matter, such as firing a rocket to Mars. However, it is impossible to ignore the complexity in software development. Its results are ephemeral, consisting of signals that control machines. The process is entirely intellectual, with all intermediate products being marginal representations of the thoughts involved. The materials that we use to create the end product are extremely volatile: user requirements of what the users have yet to see, the interoperation of the signals of other programs with our programs, and the interactions of the most complex processes yet—a team of people working together.

Because software development is a complex process, there is no shortage of complexities, and there is no panacea for them other than hard work, intelligence, and courage. Scrum is not for those who seek easy answers and simple solutions to complex problems; it is for those who understand that complex problems can only be met head on with determination and wit.

Appendix A describes how empirical processes are used to control complex processes, and how Scrum employs these empirical processes to control product development projects. When I say *control*, I don't mean control to create what we predict. I mean that we will control the process to guide the work toward the most valuable outcome possible.

Empirical Process Control

Complex problems are those that behave unpredictably, and the unpredictable manner in which they behave is unpredictable. Stated another way, a statistical sample of the operation of these processes will never yield a meaningful insight into their underlying mathematical model, and attempts at forming meaningful insight can only be made by summarizing their operation to such a degree of coarseness as to be irrelevant to understanding or managing them.

Much of our society is based on processes that work only because their degree of imprecision is acceptable. Wheels wobble, cylinders shake, brakes jitter—but all at a level that doesn't meaningfully impede our use of a car. When we build cars, we fit parts together with a degree of precision fit for the purpose and acceptable to the eye. We can manage many processes because the accuracy of the results is limited by our physical perceptions. When I build a cabinet, the materials need to be cut and joined with a precision acceptable to the human eye and suitable for a relatively static daily life.

What happens when we are building something that requires a higher degree of precision than that obtainable through averaging? What happens if any process that we devise for building cars is too imprecise for our customers, and we need to increase the level of precision? In those cases, we have to guide the process step by step ourselves, ensuring that the process converges on an acceptable degree of precision. When the convergence isn't occurring, we have to make adaptations to bring the process back into acceptable tolerances.

Laying out a process that will produce acceptable quality output over and over again is called *defined process control*. When defined process control cannot be achieved because of the complexity of the intermediate activities, something called *empirical process control* has to be employed.

> *"It is typical to adopt the defined (theoretical) modeling approach when the underlying mechanisms by which a process operates are reasonably well understood. When the process is too complicated for the defined approach, the empirical approach is the appropriate choice."*
>
> –Babatunde A. Ogunnaike and W. Harmon Ray
> *Process Dynamics, Modeling, and Control* (Oxford Univ. Press, 1994)

We try to use defined processes whenever possible, because with them we can crank up unattended production to such a quantity that the output can be priced as a commodity. However, if the commodity is of such unacceptable quality as to be unusable, if the rework is too great to make the price acceptable, or if the cost of unacceptably low yields is too high, we have to turn to and accept the higher costs of empirical process control. In the long run, making successful products the first time using empirical process control has turned out to be much cheaper than reworking many unsuccessful products using defined process control. Empirical process control has three legs underlying all of its implementations: transparency, inspection, and adaptation. *Transparency* means that the aspects of the process that affect the outcome must be visible to those controlling the process. Not only must these aspects be transparent, but also what is being seen must be known. That is, when someone inspecting a process believes that something is done, it must be equivalent to their definition of "done." In product development, asserting that functionality is done might lead someone to assume that it is cleanly coded, refactored, unit tested, built, and acceptance tested. Someone else might assume only that the code has been built. If everyone doesn't know what the definition of "done" is, the other two legs of empirical process control don't work. When someone describes something as "done," everyone must understand what "done" means.

The second leg is *inspection*. The various aspects of the process must be inspected frequently enough so that unacceptable variances in the process can be detected. The frequency of inspection has to take into consideration that all processes are changed by the act of inspection. A conundrum occurs when the required frequency of inspection exceeds the tolerance to inspection of the process. Fortunately, this doesn't seem to be true of software development. The other factor in inspection is the inspector. The inspector must possess the skills to assess what he or she is inspecting.

The third leg of empirical process control is *adaptation*. If the inspector determines from the inspection that one or more aspects of the process are outside acceptable limits and that the resulting product will be unacceptable, the inspector must adjust the process or the material being processed. The adjustment must be made as quickly as possible to minimize further deviation.

An example of an empirical process control is a code review. The code is reviewed against coding standards and industry best practices. Everyone involved in the review fully and mutually understands these standards and best practices. The code review occurs whenever someone feels that a section of code is complete. The most experienced developers review the code, and their comments and suggestions lead to the developer adjusting his or her code.

Complex Software Development

When we build software, we are building a logical set of instructions that send signals that control a machine in its interactions with other machines, humans, or nature. The level of precision required for successful software ranges from the incredible to the truly daunting. Anything can be complex. When complex things interact, the level of complexity increases tremendously. I've limited my enumeration of complexity in software development to the three most significant dimensions: requirements, technology, and people.

Simple software requirements can happen. A single customer who is the only person who will use the system can spend so much time with me that I firmly believe that I understand what he or she wants. If this customer then immediately dies, the requirements are stable and simple. No changes, no revisions, no last-minute modifications. A more common situation is when there are many customers or stakeholders (those with an interest in the software and how it works) who have different needs that change and are difficult to articulate. In most cases, these customers really start to understand what they want only when you provide them with what you and they think they want. These are complex requirements because they are not only ambiguous, but they are tentative and constantly changing.

Simple technology exists, but it is rarely used in software development. One could define software development projects as the application of advanced, not necessarily 100-percent reliable, technology to solve business problems for competitive advantage. To compound the complexity of technology, more than one piece is usually employed and the interfaces of the many are far more complex than the complexity within any single piece.

In Figure A-1, the vertical axis traces requirements complexity and the horizontal axis traces technology complexity. The intersection of these complexities defines the level of complexity of the project. Almost all current software development projects are complex. Those that are chaotic are unworkable, and some complexities must be resolved prior to starting the project.

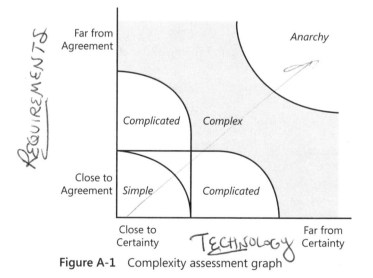

Figure A-1 Complexity assessment graph

The third dimension is the people developing the software. They all have different skills, intelligence, experience, viewpoints, attitudes, and prejudices. Every morning when they wake up, each has a different mood from the prior day, depending on his or her sleep, health, weather, neighbors, families, and what is anticipated from the day ahead. Then these people start to work together, and the complexity goes through the roof. When the third dimension of people complexity is factored in with the other two dimensions of requirements and technology, the complexity increases even more. I believe that the last "simple" project occurred in 1969 when one person from order processing at Sears Roebuck asked me to sort some cards and generate a report on an IBM 360/20. Since then, the complexity of software development projects has only gotten messier.

Scrum addresses the complexity of software development projects by implementing the inspection, adaptation, and visibility requirements of empirical process control in a set of simple practices and rules. These are described in the following sections.

Scrum: Skeleton and Heart

Scrum employs an iterative, incremental process skeleton on which hang all of its practices. Scrum's skeleton is shown in Figure A-2. The lower circle represents an iteration of development activities that occur, one after another. The output of each iteration is an increment of product. The upper circle represents the daily inspection that occurs during the iteration, where the individual team members meet to inspect each other's activities and make appropriate adaptations. Driving the iteration is a list of requirements. This cycle repeats until the project is no longer funded.

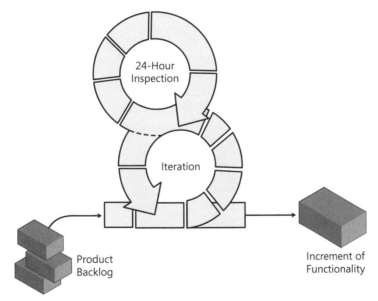

Figure A-2   Scrum skeleton

The skeleton operates this way: At the start of an iteration, the team reviews what it must do. Then it selects what it believes it can turn into an increment of potentially shippable functionality by the end of the iteration. The team is then left alone to make its best effort for the rest of the iteration. At the end of the iteration, the team presents the increment of functionality that it built so that the stakeholders can inspect it and make timely adaptations to the project.

The heart of Scrum occurs within the iteration. The team takes a look at the requirements and the technology, and evaluates each other's skills and capabilities. The team then collectively devises the best way it knows to build the functionality, modifying the approach daily as it encounters new complexities, difficulties, and surprises. The team figures out what needs to be done and determines the best way to do it. This creative process is the heart of the Scrum's productivity.

Scrum implements this iterative, incremental skeleton through three roles. I'll provide a quick overview of these people operating within the Scrum process. Then I'll describe the Scrum artifacts they use in more detail.

Scrum: Roles

There are only three Scrum roles: the Product Owner, the team, and the ScrumMaster. All management responsibilities in a project are divided between these three roles.

The Product Owner is responsible for representing the interests of everyone with a stake in the project and its resulting product. The Product Owner achieves initial and ongoing funding for the project by creating the project's initial overall requirements, return on investment objectives, and release plans. The list of requirements is called the Product Backlog. The Product Owner is responsible for using the Product Backlog to ensure that the most valuable functionality is produced first and built upon; this is achieved by frequently prioritizing the Product Backlog to queue up the most valuable requirements for the next iteration.

The team is responsible for developing functionality. Teams are self-managing, self-organizing, and cross-functional. A team is responsible for figuring out how to turn Product Backlog into an increment of functionality within an iteration, and for managing its own work to do so. The team members are collectively responsible for the success of each iteration and the project.

The ScrumMaster is responsible for the Scrum process, for teaching it to everyone involved in the project, for implementing it so that it fits within an organization's culture and still delivers the expected benefits, and for ensuring that everyone follows its rules and practices.

Scrum: Flow

A Scrum project starts with a vision of the system and a simple baseline plan of cost and time frames. The vision might be vague at first, stated in market terms rather than product terms. The vision will become clearer as the project moves forward. The Product Owner is responsible to those funding the project to deliver the vision in a manner that maximizes their return on investment. The Product Owner formulates a plan for doing so, which includes a Product Backlog. The Product Backlog is a list of functional and nonfunctional requirements that, when turned into functionality, will deliver this vision. The Product Backlog is prioritized so that the items most likely to generate value are the top priority. The Product Backlog is divided into proposed releases. This is a starting point, and the contents, priorities, and grouping of the Product Backlog into releases is expected to and usually does change the moment the project starts. Changes in the Product Backlog reflect changing business requirements and how quickly or slowly the team can transform Product Backlog into functionality.

MAX duration

All work is done in Sprints. Each Sprint is an iteration of one month. Each Sprint is initiated with a Sprint Planning meeting, where the Product Owner and team get together to collaborate about what will be done for the next Sprint. Selecting from the highest priority Product Backlog, the Product Owner tells the team what is desired, and the team tells the Product Owner how much of what is desired it believes it can turn into functionality over the next Sprint. Sprint Planning meetings cannot last longer than eight hours. They are time-boxed to avoid too much handwringing about what is possible. The goal is to get to work, not to think about working.

The Sprint Planning meeting has two parts. The first four hours are spent with the Product Owner presenting the highest priority Product Backlog to the team. The team questions him or her about the content, purpose, meaning, and intentions of the Product Backlog. When the team knows enough, but before the first four hours elapse, the team selects as much Product Backlog as it believes that it can turn into a completed increment of potentially shippable product functionality by the end of the Sprint. The team commits to the Product Owner to do its best to complete that amount of functionality.

up to 40% tasks may be defined later — evolve

During the second four hours of the Sprint Planning meeting, the team plans out the Sprint. It creates a design within which the work can be done. Because the team is responsible for managing its own work, it needs a tentative plan to start the Sprint. The tasks that this plan is composed of are placed in a Sprint Backlog; the tasks in the Sprint Backlog emerge as the Sprint evolves. At the start of the second four-hour period of the Sprint Planning meeting, the Sprint has started and the clock is ticking toward the month-long Sprint time-box.

Every day the team gets together for a 15-minute meeting called a Daily Scrum. At the Daily Scrum, each team member answers three questions:

- What have you done on this project since the last Daily Scrum meeting?

- What do you plan to do on this project between now and the next Daily Scrum meeting?

- What impediments are in the way of you meeting your commitments toward this Sprint and this project?

The purpose of the meeting is to synchronize the work of all team members daily and to schedule any meetings that the team needs to forward its progress. The team members are inspecting each other's work in light of the team's commitments, and making adaptations to optimize their chance of meeting those commitments.

demo

At the end of the Sprint, a Sprint Review meeting is held. This is a four-hour time-boxed meeting at which the team presents what has been developed during the Sprint to the Product Owner and any other stakeholders that wish to attend. This is an informal meeting, with the presentation of the functionality intended to foster collaboration about what to do next based on what the team just completed. The Product Owner and stakeholder inspect the team's work in light of projects goals, and they make adaptations to optimize their chance of reaching those goals.

After the Sprint Review and prior to the next Sprint Planning meeting, the ScrumMaster holds a Sprint Retrospective meeting with the team. At this three-hour, time-boxed meeting, the ScrumMaster encourages the team to revise, within the Scrum process framework and practices, its development process to make it more effective and enjoyable for the next Sprint.

Collectively, the Sprint Planning meeting, the Daily Scrum meeting, the Sprint Review meeting, and the Sprint Retrospective meeting implement the empirical inspection and adaptation practices within Scrum. Figure A-3 provides an illustration of the overall process.

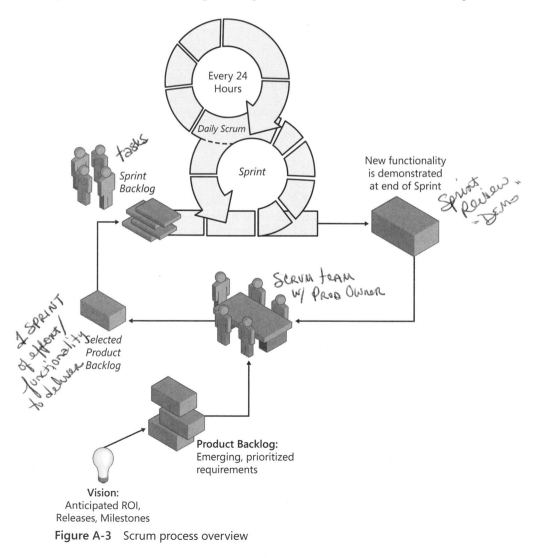

Figure A-3   Scrum process overview

Scrum: Artifacts

Scrum introduces a few new artifacts. These are used throughout Scrum and are introduced in the following sections.

Product Backlog

The requirements for the product being developed by the project or projects are listed in the Product Backlog. The Product Owner is responsible for the Product Backlog, its contents, its availability, and its prioritization. Product Backlog is never complete, and the Product Backlog in the project plan only lays out the initially known and best-understood requirements.

The Product Backlog evolves as the product and the environment in which it will be used emerge. Product Backlog is dynamic, in that management constantly changes it to identify what the product needs to be appropriate, competitive, and useful. As long as a product exists, Product Backlog also exists. An example of Product Backlog maintained on the Scrum Product Management tool, based in a spreadsheet, is shown in Figure A-4.

This spreadsheet is the Product Backlog in March 2003, from a project for developing the Scrum Project Management software. I was the Product Owner. The rows are the Product Backlog items, interspersed by Sprint and Release dividers. For instance, all the rows above Sprint 1 were worked on in that Sprint. The rows between Sprint 1 and Sprint 2 rows were done in Sprint 2. Notice that the row "Display tree view of Product Backlog, Releases, Sprints" is duplicated in Sprint 1 and Sprint 2. This is because row 10 wasn't completed in Sprint 1, so it was moved down to the Sprint 2 for completion. If I decided that it was a lower priority after Sprint 1, I could have moved it even lower down the priority list.

The first four columns are the Product Backlog item name, initial estimate, complexity factor, and adjusted estimate. The complexity factor increases the estimate because of project characteristics that reduce the productivity of the team. The next columns are the Sprints during which the Product Backlog is developed. When the Product Backlog is first thought of and entered, its estimated work is placed into the column of the Sprint that is going on at that time. The developers and I devised most of the backlog items shown before starting this project. The sole exception is row 31 ("Publish facility for entire project, publishing it as HTML Web pages"), which I didn't think of until some time during Sprint 3.

A burn-down chart shows the amount of work remaining across time. The burn-down chart is an excellent way of visualizing the correlation between the amount of work remaining at any point in time and the progress of the project team or teams in reducing this work. The intersection of a trend line for work remaining and the horizontal axis indicates the most probable completion of work at that point in time. A burn-down chart reflecting this is shown in Figure A-5. The burn-down chart helps me to "what if" the project by adding and removing functionality from the release to get a more acceptable date, or by extending the date to include more functionality. The burn-down chart is the collision of reality (work done and how fast it's being done) with what is planned, or hoped for.

Backlog Description	Initial Estimate	Adjustment Factor	Adjusted Estimate	Hours of work remaining until completion						
				1	2	3	4	5	6	7
Title Import				256	209	193	140	140	140	140
Project selection or new	3	0.2	3.6	3.6	0	0	0	0	0	0
Template Backlog for new projects	2	0.2	2.4	2.4	0	0	0	0	0	0
Create Product Backlog worksheet with formatting	3	0.2	3.6	3.6	0	0	0	0	0	0
Create Sprint Backlog worksheet with formatting	3	0.2	3.6	3.6	0	0	0	0	0	0
Display tree view of Product Backlog, Releases, Sprints	2	0.2	2.4	2.4	0	0	0	0	0	0
Sprint-1	13	0.2	15.6	16	0	0	0	0	0	0
Create a new window containing Product Backlog template	3	0.2	3.6	3.6	3.6	0	0	0	0	0
Create a new window containing Sprint Backlog template	2	0.2	2.4	2.4	2.4	0	0	0	0	0
Burndown window of Product Backlog	5	0.2	6	6	6	0	0	0	0	0
Burndown window of Sprint Backlog	1	0.2	1.2	1.2	1.2	0	0	0	0	0
Display tree view of Product Backlog, Releases, Sprints	2	0.2	2.4	2.4	2.4	0	0	0	0	0
Display burndown for selected Sprint or Release	3	0.2	3.6	3.6	3.6	0	0	0	0	0
Sprint-2	16	0.2	19.2	19	19	1.2	0	0	0	0
Automatic recalculating of values and totals	3	0.2	3.6	3.6	3.6	3.6	0	0	0	0
As changes are made to Backlog in secondary window, update burndown graph on main page	2	0.2	2.4	2.4	2.4	2.4	0	0	0	0
Hide/automatic redisplay of burndown window	3	0.2	3.6	3.6	3.6	3.6	0	0	0	0
Insert Sprint capability ... adds summing Sprint row	2	0.2	2.4	2.4	2.4	2.4	0	0	0	0
Insert Release capability adds summary row for Backlog in Sprint	1	0.2	1.2	1.2	1.2	1.2	0	0	0	0
Owner/assigned capability and columns optional	2	0.2	2.4	2.4	2.4	2.4	0	0	0	0
Print burndown graphs	1	0.2	1.2	1.2	1.2	1.2	0	0	0	0
Sprint-3	14	0.2	16.8	17	17	17	0	0	0	0
Duplicate incomplete Backlog without affecting totals	5	0.2	6	6	6	6	6	6	6	6
Note capability	6	0.2	7.2	7.2	7.2	7.2	7.2	7.2	7.2	7.2
What-if Release capability on burndown graph	15	0.2	18	18	18	18	18	18	18	18
Trend capability on burndown window	2	0.2	2.4	2.4	2.4	2.4	2.4	2.4	2.4	2.4
Publish facility for entire project, publishing it as HTML Web pages	11	0.2	13.2	0	0	13	13	13	13	13
Future Sprints	39	0.2	46.8	34	34	47	47	47	47	47
Release-1				85	70	65	47	47	47	47

Figure A-4   Product Backlog

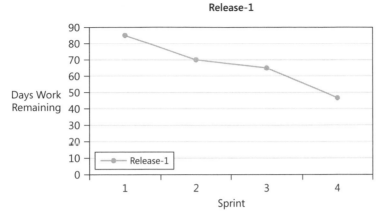

Figure A-5   Burn-down chart

The items in the Product Backlog for future Sprints are pretty coarse grained. The Product Owner hasn't had the team start to work on these items, so he or she hasn't expended the time to analyze them to more finely estimate them. Similarly, there are plenty more requirements for this product. They just haven't been thought through. This is an example of the requirements for the product emerging. I can defer building an inventory of Product Backlog until I am ready to engage a team to convert it into functionality.

task detail = 1/2 day → 2day MAX

Sprint Backlog

The Sprint Backlog defines the work, or tasks, that a team has specified for turning the Product Backlog it selected for that Sprint into an increment of potentially shippable product functionality. The team compiles an initial list of these tasks in the second part of the Sprint Planning meeting. Tasks should have enough detail so that each task takes roughly 4 to 16 hours to finish. Tasks that are of longer estimated time are used as placeholders for tasks that haven't been finely defined. Only the team can change the Sprint Backlog. The Sprint Backlog is a highly visible, real-time picture of the work that the team plans to accomplish during the Sprint. An example of a Sprint Backlog is shown in Figure A-6. The rows represent Sprint Backlog tasks. The columns on the right, labeled "Hours of Work," contain the remaining hours of work for the various days of the Sprint. Once a task is defined, the estimated number of hours remaining to complete the task is placed in the intersection of the task and the Sprint day by the person working on the task.

Task Description	Originator	Responsible	Status (Not Started/ In Progress/ Completed)	Hours of work remaining until completion											
				1	2	3	4	5	6	7	8	9	10	11	12
Meet to discuss the goals and features for Sprint 3-6	Danielle	Danielle/Sue	Completed	20	0	0	0	0	0	0	0	0	0	0	0
Move Calculations out of Crystal Reports	Jim	Allen	Not Started	8	8	8	8	8	8	8	8	8	8	8	8
Get KEG Data		Tom	Completed	12	0	0	0	0	0	0	0	0	0	0	0
Analyse KEG Data - Title		George	In Progress	24	24	24	24	12	10	10	10	10	10	10	10
Analyse KEG Data - Parcel		Tim	Completed	12	12	12	12	12	4	4	4	0	0	0	0
Analyse KEG Data - Encumbrance		Josh	In Progress							12	10	10	10	10	10
Analyse KEG Data - Contact		Danielle	In Progress	24	24	24	24	12	10	8	6	6	6	6	6
Analyse KEG Data - Facilities		Allen	In Progress	24	24	24	24	12	10	10	10	10	10	10	10
Define & build Database		Barry/Dave	In Progress	80	80	80	80	80	80	60	60	60	60	60	60
Validate the size of the KEG database		Tim	Not Started												
Look at KEG Data on the G:\		Dave	In Progress	3	3	3	3	3	3	3	3	3	3	3	3
Confirm Agreement with KEG		Sue	Not Started												
Confirm KEG Staff Availability		Tom	Not Started	1	1	1	1	1	1	1	1	1	1	1	1
Switch JDK to 1.3.1. Run all tests.		Allen	Not Started	8	8	8	8	8	8	8	8	8	8	8	8
Store PDF files in a structure		Jacquie	Completed	8	0	0	0	0	0	0	0	0	0	0	0
TopLink. Cannot get rid of netscape parser		Richard	Completed	4	0	0	0	0	0	0	0	0	0	0	0
Build test data repository		Barry	In Progress	10	10	10	10	10	10	10	10	8	8	8	8
Move application and database to Qual (incl Crystal)		Richard	Completed	4	4	4	4	4	4	4	0	0	0	0	0
Set up Crystal environment		Josh	Completed	2	2	2	2	1	1	1	0	0	0	0	0
Test App in Qual		Sue	In Progress												20
Defining sprint goal required for solution in 2002		Lynne	In Progress	40	40	40	40	40	40	40	38	38	38	38	38
Reference tables for import process		Josh	In Progress												
Build standard import exception process		Josh	In Progress									12	12	12	10
Handle multiple file imports on same page		Jacquie	Disregarded	20	15	15	15	12	12	12	12	9	0	0	0
Migrate CruiseControl Servlet to iWS 6.0 (landcc_7101) server		Allen	Not Started	4	4	4	4	4	4	4	4	4	4	4	4
Create web server for Qual on PF1D8		Allen	Completed	1	0	0	0	0	0	0	0	0	0	0	0
LTCS Disk		Danielle/ George	In Progress	12	12	12	12	8	8	8	8	8	8	8	8
Follow thru with questions about KEG data to Sue/Tom, re: Keg, LTO	Jacquie	Danielle	Completed	10	10	10	10	10	8	8	0	0	0	0	0
Map KEG data to Active Tables - see also #14	Jacquie	Jacquie/Allen	In Progress	50	50	50	50	50	50	50	50	50	50	50	50
Prepare SQL to import from KEG tables to Active Tables	Jacquie	George	In Progress	25	25	25	25	25	25	25	25	25	24	23	22

Figure A-6   Sprint Backlog

Increment of Potentially Shippable Product Functionality

Scrum requires teams to build an increment of product functionality every Sprint. This increment must be potentially shippable, because the Product Owner might choose to immediately implement the functionality. This requires the increment to consist of thoroughly tested, well-structured, and well-written code that has been built into an executable. It also requires the user operation of the functionality to be documented, either in Help files or user documentation. This is the definition of a "done" increment. It takes some development organizations a while to be capable of building something this "done."

Appendix B
More About Scrum

This appendix contains a glossary of key terms used to describe mechanisms and components of the Scrum process, as well as additional resources you can consult to broaden your knowledge of Scrum.

Scrum Terminology

Some terminology is used throughout this book. If you are new to Scrum and this terminology is unfamiliar, paper-clip this page so that you can easily refer to these terms.

- **adaptation**   Reconstituting and reprioritizing the Product Backlog at the end of a Sprint after considering the results of an inspection and changes in stakeholder needs.

- **cross-functional teams**   A self-managing team that has all the necessary skills to create a "done" increment.

- **Daily Scrum**   A daily meeting at which the Scrum Development Team gathers to inspect its progress toward the Sprint Goal and adapt its work to optimize its chances of building everything it committed to. The meeting is time-boxed to 15 minutes, during which each team member answers the following three questions: "What did I do yesterday?", "What am I going to do today?", and "Is there anything impeding my work?" The Sprint Backlog is updated before the end of the meeting to reflect the answers that team members give to these questions.

- **done (Sprint)**   As in, "This is what we *did* in this Sprint." The term defines the contents of an increment and can vary. For example, some products do not contain documentation, so the definition of "done" does not include documentation. Some organizations are incapable of building a complete piece of the product within one Sprint, so "done" actually describes something that is incomplete, but nevertheless it is consistently defined across all Sprits and all teams Sprinting. This approach works because the definition of partially "done" is known to everyone, and they also know what is left "undone" at the end of the Sprint and what remains to be done prior to shipping or using the increment(s).

- **empirical process control**   An experiential method of moving toward a goal by frequently inspecting progress and making adaptations to optimize the overall progress.

- **finished product**   Something that is of potential use to the customer; the customer can be an external consumer of the system or an internal consumer of parts of the system.

- **increment**   A complete slice, or piece, of the finished product or system that is developed by the end of an iteration, or *Sprint*.

- **inspection**   Inspecting an increment at the end of a Sprint, and adapting the priority and content of the product backlog so that the next iteration of work optimizes value.

- **iteration**   One of several successive periods of time when all the work to complete one full slice of the finished product is performed; a project consists of multiple iterations, also referred to as *Sprints*.

- **Product Backlog**   A prioritized list of functional and nonfunctional requirements and features to be developed for a new product or to be added to an existing product. The Product Backlog items of the highest priority are granular enough to be readily understood by the Scrum Team and developed into an increment within a Sprint. Lower priority Product Backlog items are progressively less well-understood and granular. Product Backlog items that are high risks are labeled as high priority to ensure that they are understood and removed early in a project. This list transcends any one release and is constantly emerging and changing.

- **Product Backlog burn-down chart**   A graph of the amount of Product Backlog work remaining in a project or program across time. The amount of work is represented by the Y axis, and the Sprint sequence is represented by the X axis. A trend line of one or more amounts of work remaining sometimes can be used to predict when a project will be complete.

- **Product Backlog grooming**   The Scrum Team spends 10 percent of each Sprint grooming the Product Backlog to meet the definition of a Product Backlog item and to ensure that it meets the requirements of the Sprint Planning Prerequisites.

- **Product Owner**   The person who is responsible for what the Scrum Team builds and for optimizing the value of it. The Product Owner is responsible for maximizing the value of the product being developed while minimizing the risk.

- **Project or Program**   The expenditure of funds to turn one or more pieces of a Product Backlog into potentially shippable functionality that can be released for use.

- **Project or Program Goal**   The reason why the Project or Program has been undertaken. When it is fulfilled, the Project or Program is "done."

- **requirements**   What the system or product must do. Requirements are subsets of features and functions.

- **retrospective**   A time-boxed meeting of four hours after the Sprint Review when the Scrum Team reviews the just-finished Sprint. After reviewing everything that worked well and things that could be improved, the team defines several changes to how it will work together for the next Sprint.

- **Scrum**   A process for managing the development and deployment of complex products that is based in empirical process control theory and stands on the core practices of iterative development, which generates increments of product by using self-managing, cross-functional teams.

- **Scrum Development Team**   The cross-functional, self-managing team that develops as much of what the Product Owner wants into an increment every Sprint.

- **ScrumMaster**   The person responsible for ensuring that everyone on the Scrum Team follows the Scrum process and rules, and who removes impediments to the success of the Scrum Team.

- **Scrum Team**   The people who work together to build increments of product every Sprint; the team consists of the Product Owner, Scrum Development Team, and ScrumMaster.

- **self-managing teams**   A group of no more than nine people who figure out how to $7 \pm 2\# \text{ OPTIMUM}$ do the work within a Sprint on their own and within the constraints of enterprise standards, guidelines, and constraints. The self-managing team can reach out for assistance or guidance, but none can be given unless the team requests it.

- **Sprint**   A Scrum iteration, normally of a one-month duration. Shorter durations can be used, but all teams within a project consistently synchronize their work using the same length iteration, which does not vary during the project.

- **Sprint Backlog**   The tasks the Scrum Development Team performs to turn Product Backlog items into a "done" increment. Many are developed during the Sprint Planning Meeting (How), but up to 40 percent might emerge during the Sprint. For a Scrum Development Team to start work on a Sprint Backlog item, the task must takes 16 hours or less to be completed.

- **Sprint Backlog burn-down chart**   A graph of the amount of Sprint Backlog work remaining in a Sprint across time. The amount of work is represented by the Y axis, and the Sprint sequence is represented by the X axis.

- **Sprint Goal**   The purpose of the Sprint. This is a statement that provides guidance to the team on why it is building the increment. The Sprint Goal is a subset of the Project or Program Goal.

- **Sprint Planning Meeting**   A meeting during which the Sprint content and the goal of the Sprint are planned. Required attendees are the Product Owner, ScrumMaster, and development team. The time-box is eight hours and is decomposed into "what" and "how" time-boxes. WITH PROD OWNER

- **Sprint Planning Meeting (Enterprise)**   A Sprint Planning Meeting of up to seven Scrum Teams that build a common, integrated increment. The Scrum Teams review the overall Product Backlog that they will work from, select Product Backlog items to minimize, and note dependencies they must remain aware of.

■ **Sprint Planning Meeting (How)**   The second four hours of the Sprint Planning Meeting, during which the Scrum Development Team figures out how it will turn the Product Backlog selected during Sprint Planning Meeting (What) into a "done" increment within the Sprint. The team usually starts by designing the work and figuring out how to do it and who will do it. As this design takes shape, tasks to turn the Product Backlog into an increment are defined. These tasks make up the Sprint Backlog. Most teams develop 60 percent of all the tasks they will do during a Sprint during this time-box. The Product Owner is present during this meeting to clarify the Product Backlog and to help the team make design decisions. If the team determines that it has too much or too little work, it can renegotiate the Product Backlog items that it will work on during the Sprint with the Product Owner.

■ **Sprint Planning Meeting (What)**   The first four hours of the Sprint Planning Meeting, during which the Product Owner goes over the highest priority Product Backlog items with the Scrum Development Team. From these high-priority items, the team selects as much as it believes it can turn into an increment in the upcoming Sprint. If the Sprint Planning Prerequisites are well formed, this meeting usually takes less than the time-box of four hours.

■ **Sprint Planning Prerequisites**   The inputs to the Sprint Planning Meeting. These include the Scrum Team's capacity for work in the upcoming Sprint and a Product Backlog decomposed to include work that is understood and can be completed within one Sprint. Enough Product Backlog must be decomposed to this degree of granularity to consume the Scrum Team's capacity.

■ **Sprint Review Meeting**   The inspection at the end of the Sprint in which the Product Owner and stakeholders review the increment and collaborate with the Scrum Development Team. This is a working session that leads to the adaptation of the Product Backlog. This meeting is not a demonstration, and preparation should be minimized to less than one hour. This meeting is time-boxed to four hours.

■ **Sprint Review Meeting (Enterprise)**   A Sprint Review Meeting of up to seven Scrum Teams that are building a common, integrated increment. The Scrum Teams show their increments and collaborate on the most appropriate adaptations.

■ **stakeholders**   People who have a vested interest in a project. All stakeholders and customers are represented by one person, the Product Owner.

■ **time-box**   A maximum amount of allotted time for accomplishing a goal or task. All work must be completed within this duration.

■ **transparency**   A degree of clarity such that, upon inspection, everything about the item or process in question can be known.

- **transparency (Daily Scrum)**   A Scrum Development Team member knows exactly what he or she is inspecting at the Daily Scrum when another member says, "I did this yesterday," because the team has defined what "did" (and "done") means for the Sprint. For instance, "I did *x* yesterday," might mean that a particular function was coded, code reviewed, unit tested, checked in, built, had the unit test hardness run against it, and had the acceptance test harness run against it.

- **transparency (increment)**   A term that indicates the Product Owner knows exactly what he or she is inspecting at the end of the Sprint because the increment meets the definition of "done" and the Product Owner understands the definition.

- **velocity**   The average amount of work a Scrum Team removes from the Product Backlog at the end of each Sprint.

These simple mechanisms are bound together by rules. The rules are similar to rules used in chess: a knight can move two spaces forward and one space to the side, but it can't land on another piece from the same side. A Scrum rule is that the team works only on the Product Backlog that it has selected for the Sprint; no new work can be added.

Scrum and Agile Books

Many books have been written about Agile techniques in general and Scrum in particular. The following list is divided into topics to help you find a title that best suits your particular area of interest.

Scrum Books

- *Agile Software Development with Scrum* by Ken Schwaber and Mike Beedle (Prentice Hall, 2001)
- *Agile Project Management with Scrum* by Ken Schwaber (Microsoft Press, 2004)

Books on Techniques Used in Scrum for Managing Product Development

- *Agile Estimating and Planning* by Mike Cohn (Prentice Hall, 2005)
- *User Stories Applied* by Mike Cohn (Prentice Hall, 2004)
- *Agile Retrospectives* by Esther Derby and Johanna Rothman (Pragmatic Bookshelf, 2006)

Books on Managing in an Agile Enterprise

- *The Five Dysfunctions of a Team* by Patrick Lencioni (Jossey-Bass, 2002)
- *The Servant Leader* by James A. Autry (Three Rivers Press, 2001)

Books on Related Theory

- *Lean Software Development* by Mary Poppendieck and Tom Poppendieck (Prentice Hall, 2003)
- *Process Dynamics, Modeling, and Control* by Babatunde A. Ogunnaike and W. Harmon Ray (Oxford University Press, 1994)

Books that Provide Insights into Agile

- *Extreme Programming Explained* by Kent Beck (Prentice Hall, 2004)
- *Agile and Iterative Development* by Craig Larman (Prentice Hall, 2003)

Books on Agile Software Engineering Techniques

- *Working Effectively with Legacy Code* by Michael Feathers (Prentice Hall, 2004)
- *Fit for Developing Software* by Rich Mugridge and Ward Cunningham (Prentice Hall, 2005)

Scrum and Agile Web Sites

- Ken Schwaber's Web site, *www.controlchaos.com*
- Mike Cohn's Web site, *www.mountaingoatsoftware.com*
- Esther Derby's Web site, *www.estherderby.com*
- ScrumAlliance Web site, *www.scrumalliance.org*
- Agile Alliance Web site, *www.agilealliance.org*

Appendix C
Example Scrum Kickoff Meeting Agenda

In this chapter:

This appendix contains a Scrum Kickoff meeting agenda from an enterprise that is in the middle of adopting Scrum. The agenda is somewhat rigorous, but no more than most Scrum meetings.

Conduct Kickoff Meeting

The Scrum implementation begins with a meeting of senior management to decide whether to go forward with the use of Scrum for product development throughout the enterprise. This is a relatively short meeting. Not much time is needed to determine whether or not everyone is on board and ready to actively participate. If they are not, this is not the meeting to use to convince them. This meeting is more of a kickoff.

The rules at this meeting are as follows:

- All cell phones must be turned off.

- No e-mail or instant messaging can be used.

- No interruptions are allowed for any purposes.

- Anyone late for the meeting or late coming back from a break has to at least pay a fine and might be excluded from the meeting, if appropriate.

If everyone can't agree to these rules, it is unlikely that the senior management group will have the stamina and determination for the impending change effort. We use the following agenda for the kickoff meeting:

- **Review how Scrum works.**   The basic Scrum process will be reviewed to ensure that everyone has the same initial understandings and uses the same language.

- **State the goals of using Scrum and changing the enterprise.**   Every project needs to have goals. These goals set a context for prioritizing project work and within which decisions will be made.

- **Review the Enterprise Transition (ETC) project and staffing.**   Review how the Scrum implementation project (ETC) will work, how problems will be detected, how change will occur, and how Scrum will be used as the process for managing the project.

- **Review changes that are likely to happen.**   Review the types of changes that can be anticipated within the enterprise.

- **Make prerequisite decisions.**   The following decisions should be made:

  - Decide the date for the first Sprint Planning meeting for ETC. It should be within one week. It can't be later than one month from the kickoff meeting.

  - Decide who will be the ScrumMaster for ETC. A senior manager who is well-connected, determined, conversant with change, and fearless is required.

  - Decide who will be the Product Owner for ETC. This needs to be the most senior executive in the enterprise, the person who is responsible for the success of the enterprise.

  - Decide who will be on the ETC team.

- **Decide to go forward.**   Once the decision to move forward has been made, the following commitments must be made:

  - We, the members of the senior management team, are responsible for using Scrum to successfully reach our goals. The senior management team is called the Enterprise Transition (ETC) project team.

  - We will go forward with using Scrum for product development and changing the enterprise to optimize itself to take advantage of Scrum.

  - There will be an Enterprise Transition project, and it will follow the Scrum process to reach the stated goals.

  - The Enterprise Transition project will be started within one month.

  - The following actions will be completed prior to the start of the Enterprise Transition project. The responsibility for completing the work belongs to the Enterprise Scrum team of senior executives. They cannot delegate their work to more than one level down.

If these or equivalent commitments can't be made at this time, consider delaying the project, with the following considerations:

  - What do you need to believe that Scrum will help you achieve your goals?

  - What do you need to believe that Scrum is appropriate for ETC?

  - If the competitiveness and effectiveness of your enterprise isn't paramount, what is?

- **Complete the follow-up actions.**   Once these decisions are made, the following actions must be initiated and completed within one month. These are the highest priority items on the initial ETC transition backlog.

  - ❑ The ETC team must attend formal Certified ScrumMaster training.

  - ❑ A method and the mechanisms for tracking enterprise change will be defined.

  - ❑ Additional initial transition backlog items must be formulated.

  - ❑ The ETC project must be initiated, as defined in the following bulleted items.

  - ❑ Communicate these decisions and what is about to happen to everyone. And then communicate them again and again. Communicate any changes. Keep everyone in the loop. Make these communications face to face.

  - ❑ Establish an enterprise vehicle, such as a Web site, that ensures everyone knows about the change.

  - ❑ Establish a mechanism that allows anyone in the enterprise to give feedback or suggestions.

  - ❑ Establish preconditions for development projects that use Scrum.

  - ❑ Establish metrics for tracking Scrum projects.

  - ❑ Establish reporting mechanisms for Scrum projects.

  - ❑ Establish a mechanism that enables anyone within the enterprise to add items to the transition backlog.

  - ❑ Measure morale.

Initial Enterprise Transition Product Backlog

This appendix describes a high-priority transition Product Backlog that should be addressed once an enterprise has decided to go forward with Scrum.

Establish Preconditions a Project Must Meet to Use Scrum

Once senior management has decided to roll out Scrum, more people and projects will want to use it than can be accommodated. It is wise at this point for certain preconditions to be established. A project must meet them before it can officially use Scrum. Some of the most important preconditions are the following ones:

- **Full-Time Team**   The core of the Scrum team must be devoted full time to the project. Although they sometimes might need the services of experts who aren't full time, trying to Scrum with part-time team members only perpetuates bad habits and undercuts the value that everyone expects.

- **ScrumMaster Training**   The ScrumMaster is supposed to lead the team and Product Owner through the change. Make sure that the ScrumMaster receives full Certified ScrumMaster training prior to the project starting. The ScrumMaster should also connect with other, more experienced ScrumMasters to mentor him or her.

- **Product Owner Training**   The Product Owner is not accustomed to managing a project throughout its entirety, Sprint by Sprint, to maximize the value of the investment. He or she needs Certified Product Owner training.

- **Team Formation Activities**   The entire team, including the Product Owner and Scrum-Master, need to form themselves into a team. There are numerous books and consultants to help you with this activity. If the Human Resources department is engaged in the Scrum process, ask it to help with procuring these resources.

- **Team Room**   The team needs a room for its Daily Scrum, and a full-time room within which they can work. This is not yet collocated space, which will be provided for them when they request it.

Establish New Metrics

Scrum metrics are very different from the metrics that most enterprises use to manage their development projects. Earlier, more traditional metrics were derived in an attempt to abstract what was happening in a project that lasted for months and months before anything was visible. In a Scrum project, team progress is visible every day within a Sprint at the Daily Scrum and through the Sprint burn-down graph. And project progress is visible every month through the Sprint Review and the Product Backlog burn-down graph.

Two primary metrics are used to track a Scrum project:

- **Return on investment (ROI)**   Prior to a project being approved, the Product Owner must calculate the ROI. As the project progresses, Sprint by Sprint, this helps management and the Product Owner evaluate whether the investment is within bounds. Unacceptable productivity by the development team could indicate that the project might be better off being cancelled.

- **Productivity**   The primary measure of productivity is a team's ability to turn Product Backlog items into shippable product functionality. We measure this for some financial value (for example, $100,000) and defect rate (number of defects, retrospectively determined). Track this metric across a large number of Sprints and projects. This metric will normalize across time, and then trends can be tracked. This metric is of little value for measuring a single Sprint because of local anomalies.

Suboptimal Metrics

There are a large number of other things that can be measured. Measuring any one of them for very long will tend to produce skewed behavior by the Product Owner or team, as they optimize to it and suboptimize other things of value. We tend to implement and use these metrics only when a problem is detected. The metric then helps us improve the problem until it is fixed. At that time, remove the metric.

Change Project Reporting

You currently have methods for tracking a project. Review all the ways that you do so. Many of them might be appropriate for a waterfall development process, but they might be inappropriate or not even available when you use Scrum. Review the mechanisms within Scrum for tracking progress, such as Sprint Reviews, Product Backlogs, and burn-down graphs. Keep only those existing reports that add value to Scrum's techniques. The added value should be greater than the cost of gathering and reporting the data.

Establish a Scrum Center

An enterprise needs to establish how Scrum will be used, how projects and teams using Scrum will fit into the organization, and the rest of the process for using Scrum. A Scrum Center uses this emerging information to train, coach, mentor, and audit project teams. The Scrum Center usually consists of trained, experienced ScrumMasters who are responsible for Scrum's effectiveness within the enterprise.

Every team struggles to get the most benefits from Scrum. The team's ScrumMaster is responsible for leading them through the transition to a point where it uses Scrum effectively. However, the ScrumMaster and team often get so embroiled in their work that they lose perspective on themselves. For this purpose, having an audit capability is useful. Someone who knows Scrum and is from outside the team needs to have a way to measure how well the team is using Scrum. These measurements are quantifications, which are always dangerous. Some teams can be doing great but quantify less well than other teams. The feel, smell, and general sense an expert outsider has of how the team is doing should confirm, or even drive, the quantification. Further coaching or mentoring can be provided to teams that need to improve.

Appendix E
Scrum Musings

Here follow some other thoughts on Scrum topics.

Value-Driven Development

Chapter 9 briefly describes how the Product Owner can use value-driven development to change the relationship between herself and the development team while retaining product quality. Let's revisit that process here and see in more detail how that value is realized.

Scrum introduces the concept of workload management to systems development. Workload management involves controlling development of functionality and release dates to optimize the value to the organization of the system being developed. This is different from work management, in which the specific tasks involved in building a system are directed.

Scrum makes workload management possible through iterative, incremental development. Development occurs in a series of short iterations of less than one month duration. An increment of functionality is done by the end of every iteration. The term "done" here means potentially shippable or able to be implemented. "Done" means complete—that is, it has been fully tested and includes user documentation.

Traditional development methodologies fully analyze and design a system before coding it. Testing usually follows the coding. It is not until the very end of the project that the system can be implemented. The opportunities for managing this workload to optimize value are limited and usually not very considerable. However, Scrum makes it possible to perform analysis, design, testing, coding, and documentation in every iteration. This provides management with many opportunities to do the following:

- Arrange the sequence in which functionality is iteratively developed so that the most valuable functionality is built first.

- Continue to rearrange the sequence of functionality development as the project progresses and business priorities change.

- Group increments of functionality into more frequent releases, allowing the business to realize early and frequent benefits.

Consider a system that will bring the organization $1,000,000 in benefits in the first two years after its implementation. Using traditional methods, the system would take one year to develop at a cost of $400,000. Scrum lets us develop and implement the system's functionality selectively and incrementally by doing the following:

1. Listing the functionality of the system, with more attention paid to the highest value and priority functionality

2. Dividing the functionality list into two releases, the first estimated to be ready six months after development begins

3. Using iterative, incremental development to complete the first release within six months for $200,000

4. Allowing benefits worth $800,000 to begin accruing after just six months, with the functionality that will deliver the remaining value scheduled to be developed during the second iteration

5. Permitting the second implementation to be deferred if it is not deemed cost effective and the benefits of the first implementation are deemed sufficient—for example, if the development cost of $200,000 for the less valuable functionality would generate only $200,000 in benefits.

In this case, the customer had an opportunity to realize $200,000 in benefits six months earlier than would otherwise have been possible. The customer also had the opportunity to choose not to spend an additional $200,000 for break-even functionality. The time and effort that would have gone into the second iteration could instead be allocated to other higher priority projects. The benefits of multiple releases are somewhat offset by implementation costs.

Strategic and competitive systems are able to gain marketplace advantage through such incremental strategies. Imagine that your competition uses traditional development approaches to prepare a single new release or business capability, but your organization uses Scrum to produce early and repeated competitive advantages. If this is the case, your organization is able to capture the advantage more effectively and thoroughly.

An additional benefit of workload management is inventory reduction. As in manufacturing, unfinished "raw goods" software inventory is an undesirable cost. The inventory might need to be reworked if it has defects. It might never even be used if production costs are too high or demand for the software evaporates. Yet traditional development methodologies amass huge inventories of analysis, design, and coding artifacts even as business changes render them obsolete. The Scrum approach minimizes the extent to which an organization accumulates such artifacts. Only artifacts that are necessary to build each iteration's increment of functionality—the highest priority functionality—are built.

Workload management is a key new role afforded by Scrum. This role is referred to as "the Product Owner." This role has responsibilities that enable an organization to realize the benefits of workload management. The Product Owner executes the responsibilities of this role through active management of an inventory called Product Backlog.

Let's look more closely at Product Backlog. Product Backlog is a simple list of requirements for the system. Each item on the list is a single line in length. Functional requirements, such as "the ability to calculate available credit," are listed along with nonfunctional requirements, such as "the capacity to handle up to 100,000 simultaneous transactions with sub-second response time." Product Backlog is often maintained in spreadsheet format so that it can be easily manipulated and interpreted.

The Product Backlog is a prioritized list. Items at the top of the list are those that will deliver the most business value. Business priorities can change over the course of the project, and consequently the order of the list can change as well. Dependent functionality, or functionality that is required to support the highest priority backlog, is of an even higher priority. An estimate of how long it will take developers to turn the functionality into an increment of potentially shippable product is included in each backlog item.

The Product Owner doesn't have to specify all the details of every entry in the Product Backlog. The Product Owner extracts requirements from the systems plan, focusing on the highest priority Product Backlog first. At first, the Product Owner needs to list only as much Product Backlog as is needed to drive the first probable release. The lower priority functionality can be itemized and delivered only when it is deemed to be the highest priority available functionality. Even then, its development can be deferred if it costs more than it is worth.

Realizing Project Benefits Early

Keeping with the theme of value, let's look at a few real-world examples of companies that used Scrum iterative development principles to increase a project's value.

Any systems development process that provides for early realization of project benefits and maximized return on investment creates value. ThoughtWorks develops systems for its customers using Scrum. In a recent study by Forrester Research, ThoughtWorks customers identified early realization of benefits as a primary reason why they were pleased with their relationship with ThoughtWorks (posted at the ThoughtWorks Web site at *http://www.thoughtworks.com/forrester_tei.pdf*).

In the previous section, I mentioned that all Scrum projects use iterative, incremental techniques. At the end of every iteration, an increment is delivered that contains all aspects of the final product, including tested code, documentation, and user help. When the application calls for more incremental product, this is also included. For instance, FDA Life Critical applications must have requirements trace ability, demonstrating how the initial requirements are implemented in the finished product. This trace ability is included in every increment delivered at the end of every iteration.

Having inspected an increment of the system at the end of an iteration, customers can choose to implement the functionality before they had planned to. TransCanada Pipelines (TCPL) in Calgary, Alberta, chose to do so after just one iteration. The project was intended to automate title change feeds from all the provinces and states that TCPL's pipelines crossed. After the first iteration, the paper feed from Alberta was automated into an XML feed with a partial database and change management screens. Because over 30 percent of all changes were from Alberta, when the customer saw this one feed working, she chose to implement it immediately. The additional cost of this early implementation and realization of benefits more than offset the cost of the implementation.

Scrum development processes create opportunities for customers. They can implement one or more increments of functionality at any time. They can also make other investment choices, such as increasing or canceling funding of the project. When they inspect what the team has developed at the end of every iteration, they have all the information they need to justify such decisions.

If good engineering practices have been used to build each increment of functionality, the cost of implementing it is relatively small. If marginal engineering practices have been employed, all defects must be fixed during the implementation cycle. Such increased implementation costs discourage customers from calling for implementations. Because of this, part of implementing a Scrum process is improving the engineering practices of the development organization. As the preceding examples demonstrate, we want the customer to be encouraged to call for early realization of benefits.

Eat Only When Hungry

Scrum software development: Eat only that for which you hunger; maintain only that which you need.

When I go to the window of a fast-food restaurant, I evaluate what I want to eat in light of how much money is in my pocket. At finer restaurants, I usually spend whatever what I want costs, because payment is flexible through the use of a credit card. But, for me, fast food is still cash only, and my choices are limited by my cash on hand.

In traditional systems development, customers identify what they want—the requ
of the system—and are told what the cost will be and the date on which the syster
delivered. In a fast-food scenario, this is analogous to driving up to the window, o
and then being told to pull over and wait for our food until a specified time. During
we could figure out how to get the money to pay for the estimated cost.

Imagine buying systems functionality for a variable cost. Scrum lets customers state the
functionality they want and how much money they want to spend. The functionality is
delivered to the customer at the end of every iteration, during which the team cooks up a way
of delivering the functionality. The customer looks at what was delivered and decides whether
he is satisfied. If the customer wants the functionality in more depth, he can order more
stuff built into the functionality in further iterations. If the functionality is pretty complicated
(like a sourdough bacon burger cooked medium well, with the bacon well done and the roll
toasted), the functionality might take several iterations before the first digestible portion is
ready. However, we still let the customer inspect the "food in progress" to maximize the
likelihood that it will be what they hunger for.

Traditionally, we list all the requirements for customer functionality and deliver all of it. This
is like a fixed-price dinner, where we get all the food even if we are full and sated after only the
appetizer. Scrum lets us state the desired functionality (we are hungry) and then order
requirements a la carte, one at a time, until we are satisfied. Because the requirements can be
prioritized, teams can iteratively deliver only increments of the requirements that are most
appetizing throughout a project.

Since we are sating the customer by delivering increments of functionality, the customer
can dictate when she is sated, or when she has spent all that she wants to, and then consume
the functionality as delivered. Customers eat what they hunger for—no more, no less.

This simple analogy, comparing systems development to dining, works not only at the
consumption level, but at the maintenance level. If we eat in "all you can eat" restaurants, we
get fat, have to buy new clothes, and our health suffers. If we consume fixed-requirements
systems, we have to maintain and enhance all the functionality, even the stuff that we infre-
quently or never use.

For Customers Only

Have any of your software development projects surprised you, either because they failed
utterly, didn't come in on time, were of low quality, or took longer to deliver than you
expected? You might want to take comfort in the knowledge that you weren't singled out and
that anyone else who initiates and funds software development projects is not better off.
Most of you share a common experience. In the political arena, you would have been "spun."
Underlying it all is the thread that your software development project team worked, at both a
conscious and unconscious level, to keep you in the dark. Even though the team knew there
were problems, it hoped against hope that everything would turn out all right.

I run a class that teaches project managers to manage projects using Scrum. Scrum software development requires you, the customer, to actively collaborate with the development teams to optimize the value you get from your investment and to get the functionality that you need to meet your objectives. In this course, there are a number of exercises to explore how Scrum project managers will facilitate this. In the exercises, a difficult project is initiated. There are many risks in the technology as well as difficult choices to be made in how to support the business goals with the technology. The point of the exercises is to create a scenario where the development teams actively collaborate with you to help you minimize your risk while maximizing your value.

Many people in these courses have excelled. However, a disturbing number of these project managers are unable to help you understand your risks and alternatives. Not because they aren't aware of them. Not because they don't know that the project might not succeed or meet your expectations. They are unable to help you because they are afraid to tell you the truth. Even while fully understanding the risks, these people will tell you that they are absolutely confident that they can deliver the project on time with what you need. Words like *certainly*, *positively*, *no problem*, *slam-dunk*, and *without a doubt* slip from their lips even though their minds and experience tell them otherwise. When I ask them why they mislead you (the customer) and don't share their true opinions with you, these people that you will entrust your success and money to say that they don't want to discourage you, that they want to put a positive spin on things, and that you wouldn't work with them if they didn't have a positive outlook. They tell me that you are so dumb that you would select someone who tells you, "No problem," if they raised the specter of risk and doubt.

I ask these people how they would feel if they were treated the same when buying something themselves. Perhaps they enter a restaurant, a very expensive restaurant, and order a steak. The waiter and the chef know that the beef is old and that it comes from a herd where mad-cow disease has been spotted. Yet, they figure that what you don't know won't hurt you, that your actual chance of becoming ill is pretty low, and that they probably will be elsewhere if you do become ill. All of them tell me that they would be furious! I ask them where they get the nerve for assessing your risks for you and gambling your money in the face of uncertainty. What I hear back is a combination of fear, uncertainty, and bad habits.

Except for the newest project managers, the software development profession has experienced a period of 20 years when it was at least difficult and many times impossible to tell the customer if the project would succeed. The customer wasn't being lied to—the project managers just didn't know. Worse, because of the process used to manage systems development, project managers didn't have any way to determine whether a project would be successful or not until well into the project and into the customer's money. They covered up the appalling truth that—in light of the low probability of success—only a desperate person would fund the project.

This has led to a state where many venture capitalists and enterprises are turning to offshore development. These peers of yours have told me a number of times that they are doing this not to reduce the cost of a successful project, but to limit their losses. If the project is going to fail anyway, it's better to lose $500,000 than $1,500,000.

Scrum provides an opportunity to turn around this unfortunate situation. Month by month all the project information is available so that customers can maximize their return on investment and optimize their risk strategies. But this happens only if the project details aren't hidden from the customer.

Although it's happening slowly and painfully, and in the wake of a history of hiding the trust, we are developing project managers who are confident of what they can and can't do with your project. Look for them. Don't look for the person who tells you what you want to hear, even though you know that what you are being promised is impossible. Don't listen to the project manager who tells you that your difficult project is "no problem" and that he is "absolutely confident."

Bidding Work

We are often asked for estimates to build a system. Even though the system is complex, we are prodded with questions like, "What will it take?" And, to our regret, the estimate—once out of our mouths—becomes a contract. I had an experience recently where a professional in another field showed me another way to deliver an estimate, and I was pleased with his approach.

The exterior of my house needed painting. I called in three painting contractors, and my experience with them might be of interest to the Scrum community. The three contractors all came to my house, apprised it, and provided estimates. The high estimate was $15,000, the middle estimate was $12,000, and the low estimate was $7,000. All were fixed-price estimates good for 30 days. No estimate took more than one hour to prepare, and I walked around the house with each contractor and answered any questions they had. I was surprised at the fixed-priced bids, since I knew my house's exterior had some unique attributes that none of the contractors had encountered previously.

My house is clad with DryVit, a highly insulating foam-board construction technique usually reserved for commercial buildings because of the skill needed to apply it. The DryVit is then covered with a proprietary sealing polymer and then given a final color coat of acrylic paint. The paint application has to be carefully applied since it tends to soak in more than other paint. So I was perplexed and somewhat uneasy that these contractors thought they could fix-bid such a complex project. Maybe they thought it was simple?

Twenty days after the last bid was submitted, I was driving home on a limited-access highway. The speed limit was 55 mph. Suddenly, an immaculate, white panel truck passed me on the left, going at least 80 miles per hour. As it disappeared, I was able to make out the name on the side, "Noe Montenegro, Professional Painting." I was impressed. Here was a guy in a hurry who nevertheless cared about appearances. When I got home, I looked up his telephone number and asked him to come over to bid on the job.

Noe was a young, intelligent man. When he came to the house, he spent time looking at the exterior before even ringing the doorbell. When I came outside, he asked very penetrating questions about the exterior, its construction, and its composition. I gave him all the material and information I had, and he left. The next day he stopped by and told me that he had been doing some research. The research had led him to understand the type of acrylic paint required for my house, as well as the difficulties and complexities of applying it. Noe said that even though he and his crew were great professional painters, they had no experience with this type of exterior and were uncomfortable submitting a fixed-price bid. Noe said that if he tried to cover his uncertainty with a high bid, it might be too high. Similarly, if he made incorrect assumptions, he might underbid the work and have to take a loss.

After talking for a while, we reached an arrangement. I would pay Noe and his crew $65 per hour plus materials for painting the front of the house. Then he would give me a fixed-price bid for the rest of the house, based on his new knowledge and experience. I felt comfortable with this because if Noe's price was too high or his competence too low, I was free to not use him after the front of the house was done. Also, I would have that increment of work done and could build on it with any other contractor.

When the job was complete, the time and material and fixed-price remainder of the work cost me $8,500—and that was for excellent workmanship. Noe even cleaned the windows. I added $1,000 to the check, as I was thoroughly impressed with his work as well as his honest approach to bidding on it. I told him that I was going to use this experience as a story. He just shrugged and said, "Thanks."

Managing Work

I previously discussed how Scrum facilitates workload management by allowing for frequent, iterative delivery of shippable functionality and by enabling customers and Product Owners to prioritize direct development of top value functionality, iteration by iteration.

Who manages the work during each iteration? The Scrum answer is: the development team! In previous chapters of the book, I've described how this happens, but I'll describe it in more detail here, with a focus on work management. The Product Owner indicates what functionality most needs to be developed. The development team identifies and organizes the tasks and work necessary to ensure the result of the iteration is a potentially shippable product. Collaborating with the Product Owners, the development team determines how much priority functionality it believes it can cover in the next iteration.

Scrum work management is a shift from traditional project management practices. These practices call for a project manager to predict and plan all the work, as well as to assign it to individuals, track its completion, and make any necessary adjustments along the way. Scrum work management, instead, follows modern lean manufacturing practices and engineered process controls used in complex development environments. Scrum teams have these characteristics:

- They are cross-functional, containing all the technical and business domain expertise to take full responsibility for moving requirements forward to become working product functionality.

- They are limited in size to maximize the speed, content, accuracy, and bandwidth of communications. Team size is up to nine people. When there are multiple teams, the teams get together to synchronize their work on a daily basis.

- They are authorized to organize themselves, to divide and assign work among themselves.

- They are enabled to add tasks required for the creation of an increment of functionality as the iteration progresses; they are not expected to be able to make perfect predictions.

For the duration of the iteration, the team has the authority to manage itself. Its main goal is to do the best that it can. Applying the technology to the requirements, the team analyzes, designs, codes, tests, and documents. At the end of the iteration, the team shows the Product Owner what it has accomplished. The team uses workstations to show the Product Owner the functionality it has created. Only real working functionality counts to the customer; interim artifacts such as models do not count.

Sometimes the team does less than it has predicted it would be able to. Sometimes the team implements the selected requirements even more deeply than it had expected it could. The important thing is that the team does the best that it can. For one iteration, the team alone wrestles functionality from complex, sometimes unstable, technology and from often-changing business requirements.

To many, it might seem risky and even foolhardy to trust the team to plan and execute its own work. However, this type of Scrum development has been successfully used in literally thousands of projects. Two types of productivity occur. First, the project manager doesn't have to try to tell the team what to do and then keep the plan up to date as changes are required. Second, the team works more effectively without having to rely on external authority for any changes.

The U.S. Marine Corps uses an approach similar to Scrum for battle situations. In *Corps Business* by David H. Freedman (HarperCollins Publishers, 2000), General Charles C. Krulak, the 31st Commandant of the USMC, describes the new "three block war" that the corps faces today: "Marines may confront the entire gamut of tactical challenges within the narrow confines of three continuous blocks." To prepare the Marines, the actual fighters, for this situation, the USMC both trains everyone extensively in all potential skills and situations that can be conceived and then advises the Marines on the context, mission, goals, and risks of every situation before they are sent in to it. But, from then on, the Marines are on their own, making their own decisions. Their officers provide as much tactical information as possible, but the ultimate decisions come from the soldiers. As General Krulak says, "On the complex, asymmetrical battlefields of the 21st century, effective decentralized control and execution will be essential to mission success."

This same type of decentralized control and execution by Scrum teams is required to success-fully cope with the complex changing requirements and complex unstable technology required for today's successful systems. These teams manage themselves based on their skills and understanding of the technical and business domains.

A Cost-Effective Alternative to Offshore Development

More of my customers have been asking me how to use Scrum to help them manage offshore development. Because offshore development undercuts many of the practices that promote Scrum productivity, I ask them why they don't just increase the productivity of their teams by thoroughly introducing agility? It seems that offshore development, with its potential for lower unit costs (dollars per programmer day), offers management hope that their losses can be reduced. Their attitude can be stated as follows: "Since the project is probably going to fail anyway, let's minimize our losses by using lower priced resources to limit our investment." A more optimistic, Scrum, way of looking at this problem is to fix the problem at home and increase the probability of success.

The Scrum process "sweet spot" occurs with teams of seven people, give or take two. These teams can be extraordinarily productive, measurements indicating a potential increase of productivity at least 35 times higher than average. I'll describe some of the circumstances that support a team of this size in achieving this level of productivity. Many inadvertent practices reduce this productivity, including scaling, so let's understand how to be as productive as possible before we introduce scaling—which reduces team productivity for such goals as quicker time to market.

High-bandwidth communication is one of the core practices of Scrum. If a team has more than nine people, they tend to need to revert to written documents and formal models to keep everyone's activities synchronized. The best communication is face to face, with communica-tions occurring through facial expression, body language, intonation, and words. When a white board is thrown in and the teams work out a design as a group, the communication bandwidth absolutely sizzles.

Until the late 1990s, many engineering practices promoted formal documentation of commu-nications, such as formal models, documentation templates, and computer-aided software engineering tools. Whenever I don't work directly with team members using face-to-face communications, however, I reduce the communication bandwidth and introduce the proba-bility of misunderstandings. As I'm writing this, I'm trying to formulate ideas, understandings, and experiences into words. When you read this, you try to understand what I'm saying within the context of your experiences and current situation. In the process of narrowing my bandwidth to words, and you trying to expand the bandwidth from words to your under-standing, a lot is lost. No matter how well I write and you read. And most of us are not superb writers and readers.

Many Scrum practices are aimed at maximizing communication bandwidth. These include the following:

- Using modeling tools and techniques only to guide thought processes while on the path to code. Models are not used to document, but to ensure the rigor of the thought process.

- Collocating teams so that any team member can readily get face to face with any other team members to talk through and diagram a problem.

- Collocating teams in open spaces to maximize the access within the team. If I want to ask a fellow team member something and leave my office, go down the hall, look in the teammate's office, and find that the person isn't there, I have both wasted time and lost the thread and depth of my thinking. I also interrupt people who don't need to be interrupted to answer my question. More than just time was wasted

- Collocating teams in open spaces so that team members can see each other, see how other teammates are doing and feeling, and hear when a conversation is occurring in which they want to participate. Privacy is easily obtained by putting on headphones.

- Keep iterations to 30 days or less. Longer iterations require communications persistence through such artificial techniques as documentation or modeling tools. If the time between learning a requirement and finishing tested code is kept to under 30 days, the problem and its solution can usually be kept in the mind.

- Keep the team size as close to seven as possible. Seven minds seem able to attain and maintain a shared mental model of a system and its representation in design and code without artificial aides such as documentation. Misunderstandings and recording time are minimized.

- Use a shared code library and rigorous coding standards so that everyone on the team can readily read and understand the system. If modeling documentation is minimized, the code literally is the design. The code must be easy to read and unambiguous. Variable naming is just one example of these standards.

- Use Scrum engineering practices so that the team always knows the status of development. Test-first development ensures that the code reflects the design and that the code is tested as soon as possible. Source code management, continuous integration, and automated testing suites find errors as quickly as possible. Refactoring keeps the design simple, elegant, and easy to debug. Not writing arcane, heroic algorithms keeps code easy to understand. All of these practices combined mean that when you think you have a working system, it really is a working system that is sustainable and maintainable. This is known as an increment of potentially shippable (implementable) product functionality.

- Hold short daily status meetings. Face to face, team members communicate status and problems with each other. At full bandwidth, the team synchronizes itself daily.

These and other Scrum practices lead to breakthrough productivity. Every scaling practice will reduce the productivity of these teams in support of other goals. Our job will be to understand how to implement these scaling practices as intelligently as possible, so that we don't throw out the baby with the bath water.

How to Use Scrum and Offshore Development

These comments apply to both offshore development and teams that are distributed by location and time zone. Offshore development benefits from the frequent inspection and adaptation provided by Scrum. There is an opportunity for this at the end of the iteration, at the iteration review. There is also an opportunity for this at each daily status meeting, called a Daily Scrum. However, distances and differences in time zones can make such coordination difficult. Regardless, frequent inspection and adaptation provide the only benefit afforded by Scrum to offshore development, so every effort should be made to comply with these Scrum practices.

One of my customers has five development sites throughout the United States. This is a reasonable time-zone difference and number of sites to synchronize through Scrum. However, the customer also has development sites in Finland and India. They are investigating opening still another development site in Bejing, China. Each site can readily have its Daily Scrum to synchronize its activities within a team.

The Scrum process uses a mechanism known as a *co-coordinating status meeting*—or *Scrum of Scrums*, or *integration Daily Scrum*—which synchronizes the work between multiple teams. It is held immediately after the team Daily Scrums, is attended by one member of each team, and coordinates the work of the teams. At these higher level coordinating meetings, the team representatives answer the same three questions that you saw listed in Appendix A. ("What have you done on this project since the last Daily Scrum meeting?", "What do you plan to do between now and the next Daily Scrum meeting?", and "What impediments are in the way of you meeting your commitments toward this Sprint and this project?") For larger organizations, multiple levels of this coordination can be used, with progressively higher levels of staff meeting less frequently than one day. The time-zone differences make planning a daily synchronizing meeting extraordinarily difficult for this organization.

Offshore development violates almost every other Scrum practice that provides high productivity and quality. This isn't unique to Scrum—it's a problem for any development process. For instance, Scrum uses incremental development, with each iteration developing a complete slice of product functionality. Offshore development can be done with the development of requirements and architecture at the customer site, and the detailed design, testing, and coding at the offshore site. Then acceptance testing and the round of bug fixes and change orders takes place. The customer must fully define all the requirements up front, building an inventory that might go obsolete as business requirements change. While the offshore developers design and code the application, the functionality also might go obsolete and become unneeded.

Another tenet of Scrum that offshore development violates is the ability for the customer to steer the project iteration by iteration, based on an inspection of each iteration's working functionality. The customer ensures that the top priority functionality is developed first and might choose not to even have lower priority functionality developed. Without this frequent collaboration between development teams and customers, much that the customer doesn't require might be built regardless and that which is built might not deliver the top business value.

Still another violation of Scrum productivity practices is the absence of full-bandwidth communication between all team members. Full-bandwidth communication ensures that nuances that are difficult to capture in documentation are captured. The moment communication occurs through documentation and models, the chance for error occurs. The larger or more complex the project, the greater the chance.

Too Large Teams

The optimal size of a Scrum team is about seven people. With this many people, experts can be combined with non-experts to foster mentoring. With this many people, it's easier to include all the skills needed to effectively produce a complete increment of code at the end of the iteration. One coder, one designer, one tester, one documenter is already four people, so the number seven is quickly reached. Fewer people are more effective, with some people even advocating team sizes of three. In my experience, smaller teams are effective only when the increment purpose is restricted. For example, the increment might not include documentation or the design work might be minimal. Or perhaps the team consists of three truly outstanding individuals with all the skills needed.

A problem that occurs more frequently is an oversized team. I recently worked with teams of 14 and 17 people while implementing the Scrum process. At first, I thought that this might be acceptable; I felt that the teams would self-organize to make the size work. They did! The teams almost immediately started dividing themselves into smaller teams. In effect, the teams said, "You, management, aren't smart enough to optimize our size, so we are going to optimize it ourselves. You gave us full authority on how to work within the iteration, and we're going to do it. We see the right thing to do, and we're going to do it."

It was hard to argue with the creativity these teams demonstrated, especially when they were right. The teams demonstrated the beauty of self-organization and emergence. They determined a flaw in the iteration setup and corrected it themselves.

But what was wrong with an oversized team? When I work with a team of seven people, I can see them bend forward to start sharing ideas. I see them exchange thoughts, work through problems, and learn from each other. When I observed these oversized teams, such an easy interchange wasn't possible. For starters, the room had to be oversized to hold all the people. When someone at the far end of the room would say something, people at the other end of the room had trouble hearing them. Because the number was so great, side conversations tended to spring up; this added to the difficulty of hearing what was being said. So much was being said and so many ideas were presented that it was impossible for the various team members to keep track of everything that was going on.

A solution to keeping track of everything could have been documentation. We could have required agenda, time slots for presenting ideas, taking meeting minutes, and providing meeting reports that everyone on the team could read. But that would undercut the value of face-to-face communications and the immediacy of intimate interaction. It would also have imposed an overhead on the entire process—exactly the opposite of what Scrum promotes.

The larger, 17-person team spotted this problem itself and divided itself into four subteams. These subteams worked on parts of the functionality that were as orthogonal as possible. Normally, parsing requirements this way is a ScrumMaster and Product Owner responsibility, but the team proved to be equal to the task. Because a perfect orthogonal solution, with perfect cohesion and no coupling, was impossible, the team—on its own—devised a solution to keep its work synchronized while minimizing collisions. Each team had its own Daily Scrum. The team then held a "Daily Scrum of Scrums." Representatives of each team met daily after the individual team Daily Scrums to synchronize work between them. They self-organized into self-coordination.

The teams presented this approach to their management and me—not for our approval (because they were using Scrum and were fully authorized to devise their own solutions), but for our information. I was amazed at their creativity. Not only had the team devised a workable solution, but also it was the same solution formally documented in the Scrum methodology for scaling development projects from the small to the large. Except the team had never seen the Scrum methodology. Working on its own, the team had reached the same optimized solution within three days.

Virtual Teams Instead of Offshore Development

I recently read that over 70 percent of all IT organizations are planning or already engaged in offshore development. I see my share of this because many of these organizations are turning to Scrum and the Scrum process for managing complex projects that Jeff Sutherland and I developed in the early 1990s. Through Scrum's iterative, incremental development practices and daily status meetings, these organizations control and coordinate their onshore and offshore activities.

I am concerned with offshore development from a Scrum values standpoint. Aside from tilting development practices back to contracts, documentation, and fixed plans, offshore development reinforces the tendency toward waterfall practices. The business domain experts are in one country, while the technology domain experts are in another. Analysis and high-level design are done in one country, while detailed design, coding and testing are done in another. The best use of Scrum teams in offshore development requires that every team works from a common Product Backlog, has all the skills to build a complete increment, and performs the complete iteration of all development activities. Development activities are not parsed among teams; Product Backlog is parsed among teams.

Certified ScrumMaster sessions are used to improve the skills and practices of Scrum practitioners who serve as Scrum project managers (*http://www.controlchaos.com/certifiedscrum*). At a recent Certified ScrumMaster session in Milan, Italy, the group kicked around the idea of Scrum versus offshore development. We were looking for a way to mitigate the damaging effects of offshore development through Scrum practices.

The conversation strayed to Open Source, a movement for collaboratively developing free software. Scrum has practices and rules for iterative, incremental development of software. Open Source has practices and rules for collaborative development of software by many individuals who rarely see each other. The ScrumMasters wondered if merging the practices of Scrum and Open Source wouldn't lead to a Scrum solution to offshore development. They wondered if this solution wouldn't be more flexible and in line with Scrum values than the manner in which offshore development is usually practiced today.

Open Source values are similar to those embraced by the Scrum movement (which you can see in detail at *http://www.agilealliance.org*):

> *"The basic idea behind open source is very simple: When programmers can read, redistribute, and modify the source code for a piece of software, the software evolves. People improve it, people adapt it, people fix bugs. And this can happen at a speed that, if one is used to the slow pace of conventional software development, seems astonishing.*
>
> *"We in the open source community have learned that this rapid evolutionary process produces better software than the traditional closed model, in which only a very few programmers can see the source and everybody else must blindly use an opaque block of bits."*
>
> *—from Open Source Initiative OSI – Welcome, www.opensource.org*

One of the largest Open Source sites, SourceForge (*http://www.sourceforge.net*) has over 64,000 active projects. Each project has its project administrator, who ensures the integrity of the project work to the project vision, ensures the internal product integrity, and forms and guides teams. This role is similar to that of the ScrumMaster. Staff for each project is selected by the project administrator from his or her pool of usual suspects—professionals who have previously successfully worked on projects with them. Additional project resources are selected from online Open Source job posting boards. On these boards, interested individuals can express a desire to join a project and the project team can select qualified applicants.

As teams form and move forward, the project administrator serves as both the Scrum Product Owner and ScrumMaster. The Product Owner is responsible for setting the project vision and prioritizing the work to deliver it. The ScrumMaster is responsible for administering the process for developing the software. The team makes progress based on individual commitments from team members, who often hold full-time jobs in addition to their Open Source project responsibilities.

We wondered if the concept of the Sprint Planning meeting and the Sprint Review meeting would help organize these projects into regular iterations that incrementally deliver functionality. The Sprint Planning meeting would allow people to commit for the next iteration based on availability and skills. The Sprint Review meeting would help the team figure out its real progress and optimize its commitments and composition.

As a result of these musings in Milan, the Certified ScrumMasters are developing a new approach to offshore development, which they refer to as "Virtual Scrum." This approach will implement many of the ideas expressed above, fusing Open Source and Scrum into a Scrum approach to offshore development. The offshore development can either be rapid and focused, using full-time teams, or the development can be asynchronous with part-time teams located in various places around the world.

Forming Cross-Functional Teams

A cross-functional team consists of people from all the disciplines necessary to accomplish the work. The entire team, not specific individuals, is responsible for the success or failure of the effort. Scrum development teams are cross-functional. They are responsible for the creation of an increment every iteration. If the increment isn't successful, the team has failed—not individuals in the team. For instance, if user documentation is part of an increment, the team collectively is responsible for that user documentation being completed as part of the increment. If it isn't there, it isn't the fault of the documentation person on the team; it is the fault of the entire team.

As the team moves forward during an iteration, its members plan and work together. They lay out the tasks that each of them will perform to successfully build the increment. People with particular expertise take a lead role in that part of the increment construction, such as the people with design expertise taking a lead in how to describe the increment's user interface. The technical writer will take a lead role in figuring out the work for building the user documentation. However, it is the responsibility of the team as a whole to complete all the work and for the completeness of the entire product.

I recently saw a team where the technical writer felt he was behind and letting the team down. He felt this way because the user documentation wasn't complete at the end of the iteration. He felt guilty and was working overtime and weekends to make up for this. This course of action was wrong and represented an incorrect understanding of the nature of a cross-functional team. He is only a member of the team, and the team is responsible for building the entire increment, documentation included. If overtime was needed to build user documentation, everyone on the team should have been working it. Then everyone on the team should have discussed how to avoid that crunch during the next iteration and how to start addressing the documentation component of the product earlier in the iteration to avoid the last-minute crunch.

Cross-functional teams usually have to be built. Most organizations don't already have them. Building such a team is difficult because it usually cuts across several embedded understandings. The first understanding is that there are areas of functional expertise, such as analysis, design, programming, testing, and documentation. People who follow a career path in each functional area are the experts and are expected to be the only people who perform this type of work. Others are deemed not capable of performing work outside their area of functional expertise. To exacerbate this problem, most organizations are accustomed to using a waterfall methodology for software development. The analysts analyze the problem and describe it; then the designers use the analysis to create a design, the programmers take the result of the design and create code, and so forth. The consequence of this is that when a cross-functional team is formed from people with such a functional orientation, they operate as a mini-waterfall within the iteration.

The analyst starts the process, performing the analysis of the problem. While the analyst is analyzing, the others try to find things to keep busy until it is their turn to act. One by one, each gets a waterfall turn to apply their expertise. Finally, the technical writer gets to start the documentation, usually with no time left.

I help teams become cross functional by asking the analyst how the other team members can help. The analyst is surely the expert, but how can the analyst direct the others. By directing the others to do analysis, the whole process is sped up, everyone is aware of the results of the analysis, and the need for analysis artifacts is minimized. If this shared work occurs throughout the iteration, the progress is more rapid and cross-functional training occurs. Everyone pitches in. The time-box of the iteration helps the team realize the benefits of this approach, since a strictly partitioned functional and waterfall approach usually fails to deliver a completed increment within the time-box.

Cross-Functional Teams and Waterfall

I was teaching a class on how to be a Scrum project manager recently. These classes are called "Certified ScrumMaster" classes. Attendees discuss how to implement Scrum into their environment. Most of the time is spent discussing the unique difficulties that are expected in the attendee's organizations. The topic of greatest interest at this class was cross-functional teams.

Scrum is iterative, producing an increment of product functionality that is potentially shippable at the end of each iteration. The people who do the work to create this increment are the people who make up the Scrum team. These teams are small, consisting of no more than nine people. This team is considered the heart of the Scrum process, and they are orders of magnitude more productive than traditional software development teams. Drawing from the principles of lean manufacturing, the teams are empowered to figure out how to do their work themselves, and then they proceed to do it. That is, they rely on creativity to generate productivity. After all, who knows better how to do the work than the people doing it?

Scrum teams are cross-functional. This means that the team consists of people with all the skills necessary to create an increment of functionality every iteration. In many instances, this means that people with analysis, design, testing, coding, and technical writing skills are put together into the team. The team selects how much work it can handle for the iteration, and then proceeds to build that functionality.

The greatest impediment to teams working together is the legacy of the waterfall process. A team that is used to waterfall development works in fits and starts. The analyst does the analysis and creates a requirements document. The designers then take over and write up the specifications document. The coder then writes the code. The tester tests the code. And, when everyone else is done, the technical writer starts on the online help and documentation. While each person does his or her work, the rest of the team sits around, waiting, doing busy work, or cleaning up previous increments.

The project managers tell the team members that they should act cross-functionally—that they should forgo the tradition of waterfall. The team might try to work together in this way, but tradition undercuts their efforts. The analyst thinks, "I'm really the only qualified person to do this, and if I don't clearly document the requirements, everyone else on the team will make mistakes!" Not only that, but the analyst has a functional manager and a career path that rewards how well she does this analysis. Even the modeling processes and tools reinforce waterfall, starting at the high level and gradually decomposing into code.

How do we get the teams to operate cross-functionally, as a team rather than as a group of individuals working in a sequential waterfall? What can management do? The answer is hard to accept: do nothing. We often think that teams consist of primitive individuals without the intelligence to figure things out on their own, that they must be told what to do. If we flip this belief and rely on the native intelligence and maturity of the individuals that make up the teams, they almost always come through. It is hard to wait for this self-organization to occur, but patience has its rewards.

The team starts the first iteration in waterfall mode and is disappointed at how little it can accomplish. Usually, at the end of the iteration the coding is incomplete and no testing or documentation has been done. The team thinks about this and realizes that it would be more efficient if the analyst were responsible for analysis but used everyone on the team as his or her "legs" to get it done. By doing so, the tester is aware of what must be tested early in the iteration as well as helping with the actual analysis. Also, since everyone is doing the work, no documentation is needed because they are already aware of the requirements. And this proceeds from analysis to design, from design to coding, and so forth. The entire team is responsible for the results of the iteration; functional specialists teach everyone how to help with their area of expertise, magnifying the productivity of the team. Consequently, everyone on the team becomes cross-trained and can fill in for one another.

Most project managers are used to telling people what to do. If a problem exists, they study it and direct people to fix it. Self-organization is much more difficult. We must wait for it to occur, and it can't be hurried. Sometimes we can help team members have insights through anecdotes, metaphors, or just conversation, but we can't make a team do something as complicated as cross-functional work by directing it to do so. The project manager can help the team get to this point by questioning it: "Gee, would you be able to do the analysis faster if everyone on the team helped, with you directing?" But the project manager can't tell the team to be cross-functional; the team must realize how to do this and do it themselves.

Index

About the Author

Ken Schwaber co-developed Scrum with Jeff Sutherland sixteen years ago. Since then he has run his own software company using Scrum and helped many others use Scrum. He is a signatory of the Agile Manifesto, and founder of the Agile Alliance and Scrum Alliance. Ken has been in the software business for over 35 years. He lives in Lexington, Massachusetts.

"Scrum is changing our internal *currency*, the actual words we use to assess engineering investments—instead of talking about hours worked, actual hours vs. planned hours, number of commitments achieved, project FTE, etc., we're talking about business value delivered. The most startling consequence, as Ken points out, is that Product Management is now reporting the status of projects, rather than engineering. Adopting Scrum continues to be a painful, impediment-exposing process—but we're delivering more business value at a faster rate than ever before."

Pat McDevitt
VP, Global Engineering
Tele Atlas

"This is the book I wish I'd had at my side when Yahoo! was first starting to use Scrum. It's the insider's guide to the profound transformation that Scrum can help an enterprise achieve. Anyone considering Scrum for the organization they work in should consider this book."

Pete Deemer
Chief Product Officer, Yahoo! Research and Development
India

What do you think of this book?

We want to hear from you!

Do you have a few minutes to participate in a brief online survey?

Microsoft is interested in hearing your feedback so we can continually improve our books and learning resources for you.

To participate in our survey, please visit:

www.microsoft.com/learning/booksurvey/

...and enter this book's ISBN-10 number (appears above barcode on back cover*). As a thank-you to survey participants in the United States and Canada, each month we'll randomly select five respondents to win one of five $100 gift certificates from a leading online merchant. At the conclusion of the survey, you can enter the drawing by providing your e-mail address, which will be used for prize notification only.

Thanks in advance for your input. Your opinion counts!

* Where to find the ISBN-10 on back cover

ISBN-13: 000-0-0000-0000-0
ISBN-10: 0-0000-0000-0

0 000000 000000

Example only. Each book has unique ISBN.